Great American Poems

The Road Not Taken, The Waste Land,
Paul Revere's Ride, and 99 Others

PRESTWICK HOUSE
LITERARY TOUCHSTONE CLASSICS™

P.O. BOX 658 • CLAYTON, DELAWARE 19938

Senior Editor: Paul Moliken

Editors: Joan Langham, Darlene Gilmore, Stephanie Polukis

Cover Design: Maria J. Mendoza

Production: Jerry Clark

Prestwick House
Literary Touchstone Classics

P.O. Box 658 • Clayton, Delaware 19938
Tel: 1.800.932.4593
Fax: 1.888.718.9333
Web: www.prestwickhouse.com

Prestwick House Teaching Units™, Activity Packs™, and Response Journals™ are the perfect complement for these editions. To purchase teaching resources for this book, visit www.prestwickhouse.com/material

This Prestwick House edition of *Great American Poems* contains poems taken from various sources in the public domain. All other poems used with permission.

ISBN 978-1-60389-071-7

Great American Poems

CONTENTS

ACKNOWLEDGMENTS

"Two Tramps in Mud Time," "The Road Not Taken," "The Death of the Hired Man," and "Fire and Ice," from THE POETRY OF ROBERT FROST edited by Edward Connery Lathem. Copyright 1969 by Henry Holt and Company. Copyright 1936 by Robert Frost, copyright 1964 by Lesley Frost Ballantine. Reprinted by permission of Henry Holt and Company, LLC.

"Poet to Bigot" from THE COLLECTED POEMS OF LANGSTON HUGHES by Langston Hughes, edited by Arnold Rampersad with David Roessel, Associate Editor, copyright © 1994 by The Estate of Langston Hughes. Used by permission of Alfred A. Knopf, a division of Random House, Inc.

"The Emperor of Ice-Cream," from THE COLLECTED POEMS OF WALLACE STEVENS by Wallace Stevens, copyright 1954 by Wallace Stevens and renewed 1982 by Holly Stevens. Used by permission of Alfred A. Knopf, a division of Random House, Inc.

"Harlem (2)," from THE COLLECTED POEMS OF LANGSTON HUGHES by Langston Hughes, edited by Arnold Rampersad with David Roessel, Associate Editor, copyright © 1994 by The Estate of Langston Hughes. Used by permission of Alfred A. Knopf, a division of Random House, Inc.

"The Negro Speaks of Rivers," from THE COLLECTED POEMS OF LANGSTON HUGHES by Langston Hughes, edited by Arnold Rampersad with David Roessel, Associate Editor, copyright © 1994 by the Estate of Langston Hughes. Used by permission of Alfred A. Knopf, a division of Random House, Inc.

All lines from "A SUPERMARKET IN CALIFORNIA" FROM COLLECTED POEMS 1947-1980 by ALLEN GINSBERG, Copyright © 1955 by Allen Ginsberg. Reprinted by permission of Harper Collins Publishers.

"Buffalo Bill's." Copyright 1923, 1951, © 1991 by the Trustees for the E. E. Cummings Trust. Copyright © 1976 by George James Firmage, "in Just-." Copyright 1923, 1951, © 1991 by the Trustees for the E. E. Cummings Trust. Copyright © 1976 by George James Firmage, from COMPLETE POEMS: 1904-1962 by E. E. Cummings, edited by George J. Firmage. Used by permission of Liveright Publishing Corporation.

"8 Fragments for Kurt Cobain," from VOID OF COURSE by Jim Carroll, copyright © 1998 by Jim Carroll. Used by permission of Viking Penguin, a division of Penguin Group (USA) Inc.

Yusef Komunyakaa, "The Whistle" from Pleasure Dome © 2001 by Yusef Komunyakaa, and reprinted by permission of Wesleyan University Press.

"The Red Wheelbarrow," "This is Just to Say" by William Carlos Williams, from COLLECTED POEMS: 1909-1939, VOLUME I, copyright © 1938 by New Directions Publishing Corp. Reprinted by permission of New Directions Publishing Corp.

"my dreams, my works, must wait till after hell" by Gwendolyn Brooks. Reprinted by Consent of Brooks Permissions.

"Her Lips are Copper Wire," from CANE by Jean Toomer. Copyright 1923 by Boni & Liveright, renewed 1951 by Jean Toomer. Used by permission of Liveright Publishing Corporation.

NOTES

What is a literary classic and why are these classic works important to the world?

A literary classic is a work of the highest excellence that has something important to say about life and/or the human condition and says it with great artistry. A classic, through its enduring presence, has withstood the test of time and is not bound by time, place, or customs. It speaks to us today as forcefully as it spoke to people one hundred or more years ago, and as forcefully as it will speak to people of future generations. For this reason, a classic is said to have universality.

This anthology has been assembled to celebrate the diversity of style and subject matter of 56 American poets, who lived between colonial times and the present. Poets in each generation added new techniques, afforded us new perspectives, and refined existing literary style to create a uniquely American genre of poetry. Regardless of the era, these poems reflect the poets' concerns, interests, political opinions, and emotions on both an individual and a universal level. Writing poetry has always provided an outlet for the patriot, the storyteller, the humorist, the rebel, the philosopher, and the songwriter to share their thoughts.

It is important to consider the historical context in which these poets lived and wrote. The 17th and 18th century poets were immersed in the colonization of America, the freedoms of the new country, and the hardships the new Americans frequently encountered. In Colonial America, poetry frequently appeared as children's verse, popular songs, ballads, Christian hymns, and elegies for public figures; these subjects would change shortly and would encompass many more themes.

In the 19th century, citizens began to explore the vast country, migrate westward, welcome immigrants from many countries, and develop a modern American culture. Prompted by the national schism of the Civil War, poetry also focused on various regional perspectives and antislavery protests, as well as marching songs, and calls to arms. The publication of poetry in newspapers and popular magazines brought it into the mainstream of American life, and made it easily accessible to the average person.

The 20th century brought about rapid and turbulent change. Two World Wars and other major conflicts, the Great Depression, the Feminist and Civil Rights Movements, the Vietnam War, and a transportation and communication revolution increased interaction among people and made the world simultaneously smaller and much larger. American poets became active in a variety of poetic movements that experimented with new techniques like imagism, modernism, surrealism, as well as abstract, found, and confessional poetry.

READING POINTERS

Reading Pointers for Sharper Insights

Poetry is a form of language organized by rhythm and structured to elicit emotions, as well as communicate ideas. It requires the reader to consider both *what* a poem is saying and *how* it is being said. The sound of a poem is frequently as important as its message; as you read, pay attention to how the poems would sound if they were read aloud. Some will crackle with thunder, and some will lull you into the peace of a quiet summer day. The subject matter of the poems in this anthology is also varied—from the consequences of war, to the beauty of a lover, to the isolation present in modern life.

A good poet uses every word in the poem purposefully; a good reader, therefore, must be sensitive to the implications of word choice. The saying, "One picture is worth a thousand words," is true, but the reverse is more pertinent: One word creates a thousand pictures. What the words *sad* or *glory* or *river* might mean to you is different from what they mean to someone else. Poetic language enables a reader to find meaning that is both rich and satisfying, troubling and uncomfortable, as well as personal and universal. A single line of poetry can convey the writer's emotions and ideas in very few words, and conciseness is one of poetry's essential elements.

In addition, because poetry is filled with literary devices, much more so than prose is, it creates images and connections in the reader's mind that each reader will understand through his or her own perspective. When you read these poems, remember that poetry conveys what no other form of literature can and that many times, *feeling* the poem is as important as *understanding* it.

The following reading pointers should help enhance your reading, your understanding, and, lastly, your enjoyment of poetry, which, ultimately, is most important.

As you read these poems, incorporate the following strategies:

Read a poem sentence-by-sentence or thought-by-thought, rather than line-by-line.

Pay attention to the punctuation and not where each line ends. While this may be difficult with authors such as H. D. or E. E. Cummings, some, like Stephen Crane or William Carlos Williams wrote poems that are composed of a single sentence or two. Many poets will use fragments—incomplete sentences—to make their points. Carl Sandburg's "Chicago," begins with the fragment, "Hog Butcher for the World..." and lists other characteristics of the city in a series of descriptive phrases, none of which are complete sentences, but which, together, allow the reader a glimpse of the enormous strength of the city.

Notice that poets change the usual order of words by putting the object before the verb, the subject after the predicate, modifiers in unusual places, etc.

Sometimes, this is done for rhyme or meter, but often, word order is altered to give the poem a flavor it would not have otherwise. While this technique might initially hinder your appreciation of a poem, a second reading will usually make the intent of the poem clear. Had Robert Frost written, "I think I know whose woods these are," instead of "Whose woods these are I think I know," the entire rhyme scheme of the poem would have been altered, but the rhythm would have remained the same. Emily Dickinson, however, writes: "Yet certain am I of the spot"; rewording it to "Yet I am certain of the spot" does not change the meaning, but does ruin the rhythm of the line.

Be prepared to make inferences and not interpret the poem literally.

Figurative language does not mean exactly what it says; rather it suggests meanings. Poets use metaphor, personification, symbolism, hyperbole, allusions, etc., to build associations and content in a very concentrated verse form. T.S. Eliot's line, "The yellow fog that rubs its back upon the window-panes," is an example of personification; the fog has no back, nor can it "rub" against anything. The imagery, however, is effective, and you should form a mental image of fog as you read the line. The title of Jean Toomer's poem, "Her lips are Copper Wire," is a metaphor, but what does it mean? The person's lips cannot be made of copper, so it is up to the reader to infer meaning from the image.

Reading a poem requires multiple readings to get a rich understanding of what the poet means to convey.

Read the poem through to familiarize yourself with the content. Don't dwell on a troublesome word or confusing passage on this first reading. Think about the title and its relationship with the poem. Try to read the poem and be receptive to its sound, which means you should read it aloud. Reread the poem aloud as many times as needed until you are able to understand it as best as you can. A great poem will not reveal itself in one reading, just as a great work of music must be heard more than once to appreciate its nuances and themes.

Upon A Wasp Chilled With Cold

By
Edward Taylor

Edward Taylor (1642-1729), the greatest Colonial poet, did not publish his bounty of finely constructed religious poems during his lifetime. Found in 1937, at Yale University, his poems were subsequently published. Taylor was born in Britain and then came to America in protest of the lack of religious freedom in England. Here he went to Harvard University. Taylor was a minister, physician, and militia leader in his town of Westfield, Massachusetts, where he remained for the rest of his life. His poetry echoes the style of the popular British Metaphysical poets. Taylor's outstanding skill and depth of religious theme are qualities that few other American poets have equaled. His poems illustrate his love and devotion to the Lord. Taylor died at the age of 87

> The bear that breathes the northern blast[†]
> Did numb, torpedo-like, a wasp
> Whose stiffened limbs encramped, lay bathing
> In Sol's[†] warm breath and shine as saving,
> Which with her hands she chafes and stands
> Rubbing her legs, shanks, thighs, and hands.
> Her pretty toes, and fingers' ends
> Nipped with this breath, she out extends
> Unto the sun, in great desire

[†]Terms marked in the text with (†) can be looked up in the Glossary for additional information.

To warm her digits at that fire.
Doth hold her temples in this state
Where pulse doth beat, and head doth ache.
Doth turn, and stretch her body small,
Doth comb her velvet capital.
As if her little brain pan were
A volume of choice precepts clear.
As if her satin jacket hot
Contained apothecary's shop
Of nature's receipts, that prevails
To remedy all her sad ails,
As if her velvet helmet high
Did turret rationality.[†]
She fans her wing up to the wind
As if her pettycoat were lined,
With reason's fleece, and hoists sails
And humming flies in thankful gales
Unto her dun curled palace hall
Her warm thanks offering for all.
Lord, clear my misted sight that I
May hence view Thy divinity,
Some sparks whereof thou up dost hasp[†]
Within this little downy wasp
In whose small corporation we
A school and a schoolmaster see,
Where we may learn, and easily find
A nimble spirit bravely mind
Her work in every limb: and lace
It up neat with a vital grace,
Acting each part though ne'er so small
Here of this fustian animal.
Till I enravished climb into
The Godhead on this ladder do,
Where all my pipes[†] inspired upraise
An heavenly music furred with praise.

An Hymn to the Evening

By

Phillis Wheatley

Phillis Wheatley (c. 1753-1784) was a poet of great skill but one most unlikely to be famous. Wheatley came to America when she was taken from her home in Gambia, Africa. Surviving the Middle Passage, she was bought and educated by a Bostonian family, who encouraged her to write. Wheatley had one volume of poetry published. Her moving verses often address religious issues to which she was devoted. As a published author, Wheatley was able to obtain her freedom. She married and had three children within five years; however, her life ended tragically. She experienced the loss of her husband through abandonment, and her children through death. Wheatley died in poverty at a boarding house. Friends knew there was another volume of verse, but it has never been discovered

Soon as the sun forsook the eastern main
The pealing thunder shook the heav'nly plain;
Majestic grandeur! From the zephyr's wing,
Exhales the incense of the blooming spring.
Soft purl the streams, the birds renew their notes,
And through the air their mingled music floats.

Through all the heav'ns what beauteous dyes are
spread!
But the west glories in the deepest red:
So may our breasts with ev'ry virtue glow,
The living temples of our God below!

17

Fill'd with the praise of him who gives the light,
And draws the sable curtains of the night,
Let placid slumbers sooth each weary mind,
At morn to wake more heav'nly, more refin'd;
So shall the labors of the day begin
More pure, more guarded from the snares of sin.

Night's leaden sceptre seals my drowsy eyes,
Then cease, my song, till fair Aurora† rise.

THE STAR-SPANGLED BANNER

By

Francis Scott Key

Francis Scott Key (1779-1843), an amateur poet, and a full-time lawyer, wrote his immortal poem, "The Star-Spangled Banner," during the War of 1812. Key was born into an aristocratic southern family in Maryland. He received his law degree at St. John's College and practiced law before becoming a district attorney. Key penned the words of "The Star-Spangled Banner" on the back of a letter at the end of a great bombardment by the British on Ft. McHenry. It became the National Anthem in 1931. His other poetry, which is religious in nature, was published posthumously in a volume called Poems of the Late Francis S. Key, Esq. *He died of pleurisy at the age of 74 at his daughter's home in Baltimore.*

> O say, can you see, by the dawn's early light,
> What so proudly we hailed at the twilight's last gleaming:
> Whose broad stripes and bright stars through the perilous fight,
>
> O'er† the ramparts we watched were so gallantly streaming?
> And the rocket's red glare, the bombs bursting in air,
> Gave proof through the night that our flag was still there;
> O say, does that star-spangled banner yet wave
> O'er the land of the free, and the home of the brave?

On the shore dimly seen through the mists of the deep,
    Where the foe's haughty host in dread silence reposes,
What is that which the breeze, o'er the towering steep
    As it fitfully blows, now conceals, now discloses?
Now it catches the gleam of the morning's first beam;
Its full glory reflected now shines on the stream;
    'Tis the star-spangled banner; Oh! long may it wave
    O'er the land of the free, and the home of the brave!

And where is that band who so vauntingly swore,
    That the havoc of war and the battle's confusion,
A home and a country should leave us no more?
    Their blood has washed out their foul footsteps' pollution;

No refuge could save the hireling and slave
From the terror of flight, or the gloom of the grave,
    And the star-spangled banner in triumph doth wave
    O'er the land of the free, and the home of the brave!

O! thus be it ever, when freemen shall stand
    Between their loved homes and the war's desolation;
Blessed with victory and peace, may the Heaven-rescued land

    Praise the power that hath made and preserved us a nation.

Then conquer we must, for our cause it is just.
And this be our motto, "In God is our trust" :
    And the star-spangled banner in triumph shall wave
    O'er the land of the free, and the home of the brave.

A Visit from St. Nicholas

By
Clement Clarke Moore

Clement Clarke Moore (1779-1863), known for the poem "A Visit from St. Nicholas" (1823), did not claim authorship until 1844. He was the only child of Benjamin Moore, a bishop in the Episcopal Church. Moore attended Columbia College, earning a Bachelor of Arts and a Master of Arts degree. Afterward, he became a professor at the General Seminary in New York. Moore's other writings were prose works and a volume of poems. He died at age 84 while at his daughter's home in Newport, Rhode Island.

'Twas The Night Before Christmas when all through the house
Not a creature was stirring, not even a mouse;
The stockings were hung by the chimney with care,
In hopes that St. Nicholas soon would be there.
The children were nestled all snug in their beds,
While visions of sugar-plums danced in their heads;

And mamma in her 'kerchief, and I in my cap,
Had just settled down for a long winter's nap,
When out on the lawn there arose such a clatter,
I sprang from the bed to see what was the matter.
Away to the window I flew like a flash,
Tore open the shutters and threw up the sash.

The moon on the breast of the new-fallen snow
Gave the lustre of mid-day to objects below,
When, what to my wondering eyes should appear,
But a miniature sleigh, and eight tiny reindeer,
With a little old driver, so lively and quick,
I knew in a moment it must be St. Nick.

More rapid than eagles his coursers they came,
And he whistled, and shouted, and called them by name;
"Now, Dasher! Now, Dancer! Now, Prancer and Vixen!
On, Comet! on Cupid! on, Donner and Blitzen!
To the top of the porch! to the top of the wall!
Now dash away! dash away! dash away all!"

As dry leaves that before the wild hurricane fly,
When they meet with an obstacle, mount to the sky,
So up to the house-top the coursers they flew,
With the sleigh full of toys, and St. Nicholas too.
And then, in a twinkling, I heard on the roof
The prancing and pawing of each little hoof.
As I drew in my hand, and was turning around,
Down the chimney St. Nicholas came with a bound.

He was dressed all in fur, from his head to his foot,
And his clothes were all tarnished with ashes and soot;
A bundle of toys he had flung on his back,
And he looked like a peddler just opening his pack.
His eyes—how they twinkled! his dimples how merry!
His cheeks were like roses, his nose like a cherry!
His droll little mouth was drawn up like a bow,
And the beard of his chin was as white as the snow;
The stump of a pipe he held tight in his teeth,
And the smoke it encircled his head like a wreath;
He had a broad face and a little round belly,
That shook, when he laughed like a bowlful of jelly.
He was chubby and plump, a right jolly old elf,
And I laughed when I saw him, in spite of myself;

A wink of his eye and a twist of his head,
Soon gave me to know I had nothing to dread;
He spoke not a word, but went straight to his work,
And filled all the stockings; then turned with a jerk,
And laying his finger aside of his nose,
And giving a nod, up the chimney he rose;
He sprang to his sleigh, to his team gave a whistle,
And away they all flew like the down of a thistle. †
But I heard him exclaim, ere he drove out of sight,

"HAPPY CHRISTMAS TO ALL,
AND TO ALL A GOOD NIGHT!"

THANATOPSIS

By
William Cullen Bryant

William Cullen Bryant (1794-1878) was born in a log cabin in Cummington, Massachusetts. At 17 years of age, Bryant wrote "Thanatopsis," which was heralded as a masterpiece of verse, even though it had been incorrectly attributed to Bryant's father. Poet Richard Wilbur proclaimed that another of Bryant's poems, "To a Waterfowl," was "America's first flawless poem." Bryant gave up a law practice to pursue a literary career, and he held the position of editor of the New York Evening Post *for nearly 50 years. In his seventies, he translated* The Iliad *and* The Odyssey. *After dedicating a statue in Central Park, Bryant fell; he died two weeks later.*

To him who, in the love of Nature, holds
Communion with her visible forms, she speaks
A various language; for his gayer hours
She has a voice of gladness, and a smile
And eloquence of beauty; and she glides
Into his darker musings, with a mild
And healing sympathy, that steals away
Their sharpness, ere he is aware. When thoughts
Of the last bitter hour† come like a blight
Over thy spirit, and sad images
Of the stern agony, and shroud, and pall,
And breathless darkness, and the narrow house†
Make thee to shudder, and grow sick at heart,—
Go forth under the open sky, and list

To Nature's teachings, while from all around—
Earth and her waters, and the depths of air—
Comes a still voice:—Yet a few days, and thee
The all-beholding sun shall see no more
In all his course; nor yet in the cold ground,
Where thy pale form was laid, with many tears,
Nor in the embrace of ocean, shall exist
Thy image. Earth, that nourished thee, shall claim
Thy growth, to be resolved to earth again;
And, lost each human trace, surrendering up
Thine individual being, shalt thou go
To mix forever with the elements;
To be a brother to the insensible rock,
And to the sluggish clod, which the rude swain
Turns with his share, and treads upon. The oak
Shall send his roots abroad, and pierce thy mold.
Yet not to thine eternal resting-place
Shalt thou retire alone—nor couldst thou wish
Couch more magnificent. Thou shalt lie down
With patriarchs of the infant world†—with kings,
The powerful of the earth—the wise, the good,
Fair forms, and hoary seers of ages past,
All in one mighty sepulchre. The hills,
Rock-ribbed, and ancient as the sun; the vales
Stretching in pensive quietness between;
The venerable woods; rivers that move
In majesty, and the complaining brooks
That make the meadows green; and, poured round all
Old Ocean's gray and melancholy waste—
Are but the solemn decorations all
Of the great tomb of man! The golden sun,
The planets, all the infinite host of heaven,
Are shining on the sad abodes of death,
Through the still lapse of ages. All that tread
The globe are but a handful to the tribes
That slumber in its bosom. Take the wings
Of morning, pierce the Barcan wilderness, †
Or lose thyself in the continuous woods
Where rolls the Oregon† and hears no sound
Save his own dashings—yet the dead are there;
And millions in those solitudes, since first
The flight of years began, have laid them down

In their last sleep—the dead reign there alone!
So shalt thou rest, and what if thou withdraw
In silence from the living; and no friend
Take note of thy departure? All that breathe
Will share thy destiny. The gay will laugh
When thou art gone, the solemn brood of care
Plod on, and each one as before will chase
His favorite phantom; yet all these shall leave
Their mirth and their employments, and shall come
And make their bed with thee. As the long train
Of ages glide away, the sons of men—
The youth in life's green spring, and he who goes
In the full strength of years, matron and maid,
And the sweet babe, and the gray-headed man—
Shall one by one be gathered to thy side,
By those, who in their turn shall follow them.

So live, that when thy summons comes to join
The innumerable caravan that moves
To that mysterious realm, where each shall take
His chamber in the silent halls of death,
Thou go not, like the quarry slave at night,
Scourged to his dungeon, but, sustained and soothed
By an unfaltering trust, approach thy grave
Like one who wraps the drapery of his couch
About him, and lies down to pleasant dreams.

PAUL REVERE'S RIDE

By

Henry Wadsworth Longfellow

Henry Wadsworth Longfellow (1807-1882) was one of the Schoolroom Poets. He was the first American writer to have his bust displayed in Westminster Abbey. Longfellow was reared in Portland, Maine. He went to Bowdoin College where his close associates were the future President of the United States, Franklin Pierce, and Nathaniel Hawthorne. Besides being a poet, Longfellow was a professor of languages at Harvard, a world traveler, and a translator. Readers remember him most for his rhythmic and easy lyric poetry, but his greatest work is often overlooked—some coming out of the tragic deaths of both of his wives. In his day, Longfellow was one of the most popular living poets. "Paul Revere's Ride" was written before the Civil War, highlighting the patriotism and resolution of the Revolutionary citizens. Longfellow died at home of peritonitis at the age of 75.

Listen, my children, and you shall hear
Of the midnight ride of Paul Revere,
On the eighteenth of April, in Seventy-five;
Hardly a man is now alive
Who remembers that famous day and year.

He said to his friend, "If the British march
By land or sea from the town to-night,
Hang a lantern aloft in the belfry arch
Of the North Church† tower as a signal light,—
One, if by land, and two, if by sea;

And I on the opposite shore will be,
Ready to ride and spread the alarm
Through every Middlesex† village and farm,
For the country folk to be up and to arm."

Then he said, "Good-night!" and with muffled oar
Silently rowed to the Charlestown† shore,
Just as the moon rose over the bay,
Where swinging wide at her moorings lay
The Somerset, British man-of-war;
A phantom ship, with each mast and spar
Across the moon like a prison bar,
And a huge black hulk, that was magnified
By its own reflection in the tide.

Meanwhile, his friend, through alley and street,
Wanders and watches, with eager ears,
Till in the silence around him he hears
The muster of men at the barrack door,
The sound of arms, and the tramp of feet,
And the measured tread of the grenadiers,
Marching down to their boats on the shore.

Then he climbed the tower of the Old North Church,
By the wooden stairs, with stealthy tread,
To the belfry-chamber overhead,
And startled the pigeons from their perch
On the sombre rafters, that round him made
Masses and moving shapes of shade,—
By the trembling ladder, steep and tall,
To the highest window in the wall,
Where he paused to listen and look down
A moment on the roofs of the town,
And the moonlight flowing over all.

Beneath, in the churchyard, lay the dead,
In their night encampment on the hill,
Wrapped in silence so deep and still
That he could hear, like a sentinel's tread,
The watchful night-wind, as it went
Creeping along from tent to tent,
And seeming to whisper, "All is well!"

A moment only he feels the spell
Of the place and the hour, and the secret dread
Of the lonely belfry and the dead;
For suddenly all his thoughts are bent
On a shadowy something far away,
Where the river widens to meet the bay,—
A line of black that bends and floats
On the rising tide, like a bridge of boats.

Meanwhile, impatient to mount and ride,
Booted and spurred, with a heavy stride
On the opposite shore walked Paul Revere.
Now he patted his horse's side,
Now he gazed at the landscape far and near,
Then, impetuous, stamped the earth,
And turned and tightened his saddle girth;
But mostly he watched with eager search
The belfry-tower of the Old North Church,
As it rose above the graves on the hill,
Lonely and spectral and sombre and still.
And lo! as he looks, on the belfry's height
A glimmer, and then a gleam of light!
He springs to the saddle, the bridle he turns,
But lingers and gazes, till full on his sight
A second lamp in the belfry burns.

A hurry of hoofs in a village street,
A shape in the moonlight, a bulk in the dark,
And beneath, from the pebbles, in passing, a spark
Struck out by a steed flying fearless and fleet;
That was all! And yet, through the gloom and the light,
The fate of a nation was riding that night;
And the spark struck out by that steed, in his flight,
Kindled the land into flame with its heat.

He has left the village and mounted the steep,
And beneath him, tranquil and broad and deep,
Is the Mystic,[†] meeting the ocean tides;
And under the alders that skirt its edge,
Now soft on the sand, now loud on the ledge,
Is heard the tramp of his steed as he rides.

It was twelve by the village clock
When he crossed the bridge into Medford town.
He heard the crowing of the cock,
And the barking of the farmer's dog,
And felt the damp of the river fog,
That rises after the sun goes down.

It was one by the village clock,
When he galloped into Lexington.[†]
He saw the gilded weathercock
Swim in the moonlight as he passed,
And the meeting-house windows, blank and bare,
Gaze at him with a spectral glare,
As if they already stood aghast
At the bloody work they would look upon.

It was two by the village clock,
When he came to the bridge in Concord[†] town.
He heard the bleating of the flock,
And the twitter of birds among the trees,
And felt the breath of the morning breeze
Blowing over the meadow brown.
And one was safe and asleep in his bed
Who at the bridge would be first to fall,
Who that day would be lying dead,
Pierced by a British musket ball.

You know the rest. In the books you have read,
How the British Regulars fired and fled,—
How the farmers gave them ball for ball,[†]
From behind each fence and farm-yard wall,
Chasing the red-coats down the lane,
Then crossing the fields to emerge again
Under the trees at the turn of the road,
And only pausing to fire and load.

So through the night rode Paul Revere;
And so through the night went his cry of alarm
To every Middlesex village and farm,—
A cry of defiance, and not of fear,
A voice in the darkness, a knock at the door,
And a word that shall echo forever more!
For, borne on the night-wind of the Past,
Through all our history, to the last,
In the hour of darkness and peril and need,
The people will waken and listen to hear
The hurrying hoof-beats of that steed,
And the midnight message of Paul Revere.

THE CHILDREN'S HOUR

By
Henry Wadsworth Longfellow

Between the dark and the daylight,
    When the night is beginning to lower,
Comes a pause in the day's occupations,
    That is known as the Children's Hour.

I hear in the chamber above me
    The patter of little feet,
The sound of a door that is opened,
    And voices soft and sweet.

From my study I see in the lamplight,
    Descending the broad hall stair,
Grave Alice,[†] and laughing Allegra,[†]
    And Edith[†] with golden hair.

They whisper, and then a silence:
    Yet I know by their merry eyes
They are plotting and planning together
    To take me by surprise.

A sudden rush from the stairway,
    A sudden raid from the hall!
By three doors left unguarded
    They enter my castle wall!
They climb up into my turret
    O'er the arms and back of my chair;
If I try to escape, they surround me;
    They seem to be everywhere.

They almost devour me with kisses,
　　Their arms about me entwine,
Till I think of the Bishop of Bingen[†]
　　In his Mouse-Tower on the Rhine![†]

Do you think, O blue-eyed banditti,
　　Because you have scaled the wall,
Such an old mustache as I am
　　Is not a match for you all!

I have you fast in my fortress,
　　And will not let you depart,
But put you down into the dungeon
　　In the round-tower of my heart.

And there will I keep you forever,
　　Yes, forever, and a day,
Till the walls shall crumble to ruin,
　　And moulder in dust away!

THE VILLAGE BLACKSMITH

By
Henry Wadsworth Longfellow

Under a spreading chestnut-tree
    The village smithy stands;
The smith, a mighty man is he,
    With large and sinewy hands;
And the muscles of his brawny arms
    Are strong as iron bands.

His hair is crisp, and black, and long,
    His face is like the tan;
His brow is wet with honest sweat,
    He earns whate'er he can,
And looks the whole world in the face,
    For he owes not any man.

Week in, week out, from morn till night,
    You can hear his bellows blow;
You can hear him swing his heavy sledge,
    With measured beat and slow,
Like a sexton ringing the village bell,
    When the evening sun is low.
And children coming home from school
    Look in at the open door;
They love to see the flaming forge,
    And hear the bellows roar,
And catch the burning sparks that fly
    Like chaff from a threshing-floor.[†]

He goes on Sunday to the church,
  And sits among his boys;
He hears the parson pray and preach,
  He hears his daughter's voice,
Singing in the village choir,
  And it makes his heart rejoice.

It sounds to him like her mother's voice,
  Singing in Paradise!
He needs must think of her once more,
  How in the grave she lies;
And with his hard, rough hand he wipes
  A tear out of his eyes.

Toiling,—rejoicing,—sorrowing,
  Onward through life he goes;
Each morning sees some task begin,
  Each evening sees it close;
Something attempted, something done,
  Has earned a night's repose.

Thanks, thanks to thee, my worthy friend,
  For the lesson thou hast taught!
Thus at the flaming forge of life
  Our fortunes must be wrought;
Thus on its sounding anvil shaped
  Each burning deed and thought.

THE WRECK OF THE HESPERUS

By

Henry Wadsworth Longfellow

It was the schooner Hesperus,
    That sailed the wintry sea;
And the skipper had taken his little daughter,
    To bear him company.

Blue were her eyes as the fairy-flax,[†]
    Her cheeks like the dawn of day,
And her bosom white as the hawthorn buds,
    That ope in the month of May.

The skipper he stood beside the helm,
    His pipe was in his month,
And he watched how the veering flaw did blow
    The smoke now West, now South.

Then up and spake an old Sailor,
    Had sailed to the Spanish Main,[†]
"I pray thee, put into yonder port,
    For I fear a hurricane.

"Last night, the moon had a golden ring,
    And to-night no moon we see!"
The skipper, he blew a whiff from his pipe,
    And a scornful laugh laughed he.

Colder and louder blew the wind,
    A gale from the Northeast,
The snow fell hissing in the brine,
    And the billows frothed like yeast.

Down came the storm, and smote amain[†]
    The vessel in its strength;
She shuddered and paused, like a frighted steed,
    Then leaped her cable's length.

"Come hither! come hither! my little daughter,
　　And do not tremble so;
For I can weather the roughest gale
　　That ever wind did blow."

He wrapped her warm in his seaman's coat
　　Against the stinging blast;
He cut a rope from a broken spar,
　　And bound her to the mast.

"O father! I hear the church-bells ring,
　　O say, what may it be?"
" 'Tis a fog-bell on a rock-bound coast!"—
　　And he steered for the open sea.

"O father! I hear the sound of guns,
　　O say, what may it be?"
"Some ship in distress, that cannot live
　　In such an angry sea!"

"O father! I see a gleaming light
　　O say, what may it be?"
But the father answered never a word,
　　A frozen corpse was he.

Lashed to the helm, all stiff and stark,
　　With his face turned to the skies,
The lantern gleamed through the gleaming snow
　　On his fixed and glassy eyes.

Then the maiden clasped her hands and prayed
　　That saved she might be;
And she thought of Christ, who stilled the wave,
　　On the Lake of Galilee.[†]

And fast through the midnight dark and drear,
　　Through the whistling sleet and snow,
Like a sheeted ghost, the vessel swept
　　Tow'rds the reef of Norman's Woe.[†]

And ever the fitful gusts between
    A sound came from the land;
It was the sound of the trampling surf
    On the rocks and the hard sea-sand.

The breakers were right beneath her bows,
    She drifted a dreary wreck,
And a whooping billow swept the crew
    Like icicles from her deck.

She struck where the white and fleecy waves
    Looked soft as carded wool,[†]
But the cruel rocks, they gored her side
    Like the horns of an angry bull.

Her rattling shrouds, all sheathed in ice,
    With the masts went by the board;
Like a vessel of glass, she stove and sank,
    Ho! ho! the breakers roared!

At daybreak, on the bleak sea-beach,
    A fisherman stood aghast,
To see the form of a maiden fair,
    Lashed close to a drifting mast.

The salt sea was frozen on her breast,
    The salt tears in her eyes;
And he saw her hair, like the brown sea-weed,
    On the billows fall and rise.

Such was the wreck of the Hesperus,
    In the midnight and the snow!
Christ save us all from a death like this,
    On the reef of Norman's Woe!

BARBARA FRIETCHIE

By

John Greenleaf Whittier

John Greenleaf Whittier (1807-1892), one of the Schoolroom Poets, was also the premiere literary spokesman for abolition. Born in Haverhill, Massachusetts, into a strict Quaker home, Whittier's strong religious views influenced his entire life. Without formal training, but influenced by Robert Burns's poetry, Whittier was a prolific writer of poetry and prose essays, publishing 30 volumes of work. His poem, "Ichabod" (1850), deals with the Compromise of 1850, and his book, Snow-Bound (1866), deals with the seclusion produced by a New England blizzard. Whittier was not strong mentally or physically; nevertheless, he made an enduring mark on American life and literature. He died in New Hampshire while visiting a friend.

Up from the meadows rich with corn,
Clear in the cool September morn,

The clustered spires of Frederick[†] stand
Green-walled by the hills of Maryland.

Round about them orchards sweep,
Apple and peach tree fruited deep,

Fair as the garden of the Lord
To the eyes of the famished rebel horde,

On that pleasant morn of the early fall
When Lee[†] marched over the mountain-wall;

Over the mountains winding down,
Horse and foot, into Frederick town.

Forty flags with their silver stars,
Forty flags with their crimson bars,

Flapped in the morning wind: the sun
Of noon looked down, and saw not one.

Up rose old Barbara Frietchie then,
Bowed with her fourscore years and ten;[†]

Bravest of all in Frederick town,
She took up the flag the men hauled down;

In her attic window the staff she set,
To show that one heart was loyal yet,

Up the street came the rebel tread,
Stonewall Jackson[†] riding ahead.

Under his slouched hat left and right
He glanced; the old flag met his sight.

"Halt!"—the dust-brown ranks stood fast.
"Fire!"—out blazed the rifle-blast.

It shivered the window, pane and sash;
It rent the banner with seam and gash.

Quick, as it fell, from the broken staff
Dame Barbara snatched the silken scarf.

She leaned far out on the window-sill,
And shook it forth with a royal will.

"Shoot, if you must, this old gray head,
But spare your country's flag," she said.

A shade of sadness, a blush of shame,
Over the face of the leader came;

The nobler nature within him stirred
To life at that woman's deed and word;

"Who touches a hair of yon gray head
Dies like a dog! March on!" he said.

All day long through Frederick street
Sounded the tread of marching feet:

All day long that free flag tost
Over the heads of the rebel host.

Ever its torn folds rose and fell
On the loyal winds that loved it well;

And through the hill-gaps sunset light
Shone over it with a warm good-night.

Barbara Frietchie's work is o'er,
And the Rebel[†] rides on his raids nor more.

Honor to her! and let a tear
Fall, for her sake, on Stonewall's bier.

Over Barbara Frietchie's grave,
Flag of Freedom and Union, wave!

Peace and order and beauty draw
Round thy symbol of light and law;

And ever the stars above look down
On thy stars below in Frederick town!

ANNABEL LEE

By
Edgar Allan Poe

Edgar Allan Poe (1809-1849) was known as one of the three Romantic pessimists. His short stories and poems revolutionized American literature. Orphaned at a young age, Poe was adopted by the wealthy Allan family of Virginia. During his life, many women influenced him; several died of tuberculosis. This disease and death dominated many of his works. Although brilliant and extremely talented, Poe could barely make a living through his writing, living in poverty his entire life. Readers often view Poe as a wild eccentric, but as a young man he was social and well liked. Poe developed the short story into an art form, set the standard for critical evaluation, and wrote unusual and haunting poetry. His life ended tragically when he was found unconscious in a ditch in Baltimore, and he died several days later of a mysterious illness at the age of 49.

> It was many and many a year ago,
>   In this kingdom by the sea,
> That a maiden there lived whom you may know
>   By the name of Annabel Lee;[†]
> And this maiden she lived with no other thought
>   Than to love and be loved by me.

I was a child, and *she* was a child,
    In this kingdom by the sea:
But we loved with a love that was more than love—
    I and my Annabel Lee;
With a love that the winged seraphs in heaven[†]
    Coveted her and me.

And that was the reason that, long ago,
    In this kingdom by the sea,
A wind blew out of a cloud, chilling
    My beautiful Annabel Lee,
So that her high-born kinsmen[†] came
    And bore her away from me,
To shut her up in a sepulcher
    In this kingdom by the sea.

The angels, not half so happy in heaven,
    Went envying her and me—
Yes! that was the reason (as all men know,
    In this kingdom by the sea)
That a wind blew out of a cloud by night,
    Chilling and killing my Annabel Lee.

But our love it was stronger by far than the love
    Of those that were older than we—
    Of many far wiser than we—
And neither the angels in heaven above,
    Nor the demons down under the sea,
Can ever dissever my soul from the soul
    Of the beautiful Annabel Lee.

For the moon never beams, without bringing me dreams
    Of the beautiful Annabel Lee;
And the stars never rise, but I feel the bright eyes
    Of the beautiful Annabel Lee;
And so, all the night tide, I lie down by the side
Of my darling—my darling—my life and my bride,
    In her sepulcher there by the sea,
    In her tomb by the sounding sea.

THE BELLS

By
Edgar Allan Poe

I

HEAR the sledges with the bells—
Silver bells!
What a world of merriment their melody foretells!
How they tinkle, tinkle, tinkle,
In the icy air of night!
While the stars that oversprinkle
All the heavens, seem to twinkle
With a crystalline delight;
Keeping time, time, time,
In a sort of Runic rhyme,[†]
To the tintinnabulation that so musically wells
From the bells, bells, bells, bells,
Bells, bells, bells—
From the jingling and the tinkling of the bells.

II

Hear the mellow wedding-bells—
Golden bells!
What a world of happiness their harmony foretells!
Through the balmy air of night
How they ring out their delight!—
From the molten-golden notes,
And all in tune,
What a liquid ditty floats
To the turtle-dove that listens, while she gloats
On the moon!
Oh, from out the sounding cells,
What a gust of euphony voluminously wells!
How it swells!
How it dwells

On the Future!—how it tells
Of rapture that impels
To the swinging and the ringing
Of the bells, bells, bells—
Of the bells, bells, bells, bells,
Bells, bells, bells—
To the rhyming and the chiming of the bells!

III

Hear the loud alarum bells—
Brazen bells!
What a tale of terror, now, their turbulency tells!
In the startled ear of night
How they scream out their affright!
Too much horrified to speak,
They can only shriek, shriek,
Out of tune,
In a clamorous appealing to the mercy of the fire,
In a mad expostulation with the deaf and frantic fire,
Leaping higher, higher, higher,
With a desperate desire,
And a resolute endeavor,
Now—now to sit or never,
By the side of the pale-faced moon.
Oh, the bells, bells, bells!
What a tale their terror tells
Of Despair!
How they clang, and clash, and roar!
What a horror they outpour
On the bosom of the palpitating air!
Yet the ear, it fully knows,
By the twanging,
And the clanging,
How the danger ebbs and flows;
Yet the ear distinctly tells,
In the jangling,
And the wrangling,
How the danger sinks and swells,
By the sinking of the swelling in the anger of the bells—
Of the bells—

Of the bells, bells, bells, bells,
Bells, bells, bells—
In the clamor and the clangor of the bells!

IV

Hear the tolling of the bells—
Iron bells!
What a world of solemn thought their monody compels!
In a silence of the night,
How we shiver with affright
At the melancholy menace of their tone!
For every sound that floats
From the rust within their throats
Is a groan.
And the people—ah, the people—
They that dwell up in the steeple,
All alone,
And who, tolling, tolling, tolling,
In that muffled monotone,
Feel a glory in so rolling
On the human heart a stone—
They are neither man nor woman—
They are neither brute nor human—
They are Ghouls:—
And their king it is who tolls:—
And he rolls, rolls, rolls,
Rolls
A paean from the bells!
And his merry bosom swells
With the paean of the bells!
And he dances, and he yells;
Keeping time, time, time
In a sort of Runic rhyme,
To the paean of the bells:—
Of the bells:
Keeping time, time, time,
In a sort of Runic rhyme,
To the throbbing of the bells—
Of the bells, bells, bells:—
To the sobbing of the bells:—

Keeping time, time, time,
As he knells, knells, knells,
In a happy Runic rhyme,
To the rolling of the bells—
Of the bells, bells, bells:—
To the tolling of the bells—
Of the bells, bells, bells, bells,
Bells, bells, bells—
To the moaning and the groaning of the bells.

THE RAVEN

By
Edgar Allan Poe

Once upon a midnight dreary, while I pondered weak and weary,
Over many a quaint and curious volume of forgotten lore, †
While I nodded, nearly napping, suddenly there came a tapping,
As of some one gently rapping, rapping at my chamber door.
" 'Tis some visitor," I muttered, "tapping at my chamber door—
      Only this, and nothing more."

Ah, distinctly I remember it was in the bleak December;
And each separate dying ember† wrought its ghost upon the floor.
Eagerly I wished the morrow;—vainly I had sought to borrow
From my books surcease of sorrow—sorrow for the lost Lenore—
For the rare and radiant maiden whom the angels named Lenore—
      Nameless here for evermore.

And the silken, sad, uncertain rustling of each purple curtain
Thrilled me—filled me with fantastic terrors never felt before;
So that now, to still the beating of my heart, I stood repeating
" 'Tis some visitor entreating entrance at my chamber door—
Some late visitor entreating entrance at my chamber door;—
      This it is, and nothing more,"

Presently my heart grew stronger; hesitating then no longer,
"Sir," said I, "or Madam, truly your forgiveness I implore;
But the fact is I was napping, and so gently you came rapping,
And so faintly you came tapping, tapping at my chamber door,
That I scarce was sure I heard you"—here I opened wide the door;—
      Darkness there and nothing more.

Deep into that darkness peering, long I stood there wondering, fearing,
Doubting, dreaming dreams no mortal ever dared to dream to dream before;
But the silence was unbroken, and the darkness gave no token,
And the only word there spoken was the whispered word, "Lenore!"
This I whispered, and an echo murmured back the word "Lenore!"
      Merely this and nothing more.

Back into the chamber turning, all my soul within me burning,
Soon again I heard a tapping somewhat louder than before.
"Surely," said I, "surely that is something at my window lattice;
Let me see, then, what thereat is, and this mystery explore—
Let my heart be still a moment and this mystery explore;—
     'Tis the wind and nothing more!"

Open here I flung the shutter, when, with many a flirt and flutter,
In there stepped a stately raven of the saintly days of yore.
Not the least obeisance made he; not an instant stopped or stayed he;
But, with mien of lord or lady, perched above my chamber door—
Perched upon a bust of Pallas† just above my chamber door—
     Perched, and sat, and nothing more.

Then this ebony bird beguiling my sad fancy into smiling,
By the grave and stern decorum of the countenance it wore,
"Though thy crest be shorn and shaven, thou," I said, "art sure no craven,
Ghastly grim and ancient raven wandering from the Nightly shore—
Tell me what thy lordly name is on the Night's Plutonian shore!†"
     Quoth the raven, "Nevermore."

Much I marvelled this ungainly fowl to hear discourse so plainly,
Though its answer little meaning—little relevancy bore;
For we cannot help agreeing that no living human being
Ever yet was blessed with seeing bird above his chamber door—
Bird or beast above the sculptured bust above his chamber door,
     With such name as "Nevermore."

But the raven, sitting lonely on the placid bust, spoke only
That one word, as if his soul in that one word he did outpour.
Nothing further then he uttered—not a feather then he fluttered—
Till I scarcely more than muttered "Other friends have flown before—
On the morrow *he* will leave me, as my hopes have flown before."
     Then the bird said "Nevermore."

Startled at the stillness broken by reply so aptly spoken,
"Doubtless," said I, "what it utters is its only stock and store,
Caught from some unhappy master whom unmerciful disaster
Followed fast and followed faster till his songs one burden bore—
Till the dirges of his hope that melancholy burden bore
     Of 'Never-nevermore.'"

But the Raven still beguiling all my sad soul into smiling,
Straight I wheeled a cushioned seat in front of bird and bust and door;
Then, upon the velvet sinking, I betook myself to linking
Fancy unto fancy, thinking what this ominous bird of yore—
What this grim, ungainly, gaunt, and ominous bird of yore
      Meant in croaking "Nevermore."

This I sat engaged in guessing, but no syllable expressing
To the fowl whose fiery eyes now burned into my bosom's core;
This and more I sat divining, with my head at ease reclining
On the cushion's velvet violet lining that the lamp-light gloated o'er,
But whose velvet violet lining with the lamp-light gloating o'er,
      She shall press, ah, nevermore!

Then, methought, the air grew denser, perfumed from an unseen censer[†]
Swung by Seraphim[†] whose foot-falls tinkled on the tufted floor.
"Wretch," I cried, "thy God hath lent thee—by these angels he has sent thee
Respite—respite and nepenthe[†] from the memories of Lenore;
Quaff, oh quaff this kind nepenthe and forget this lost Lenore!"
      Quoth the raven, "Nevermore."

"Prophet!" said I, "thing of evil!—prophet still, if bird or devil!—
Whether Tempter[†] sent, or whether tempest tossed thee here ashore,
Desolate yet all undaunted, on this desert land enchanted—
On this home by Horror haunted—tell me truly, I implore—
Is there—*is there* balm in Gilead?[†]—tell me—tell me, I implore!"
      Quoth the raven, "Nevermore."

"Prophet!' said I, "thing of evil!—prophet still, if bird or devil!
By that Heaven that bends above us—by that God we both adore—
Tell this soul with sorrow laden if, within the distant Aidenn,[†]
It shall clasp a sainted maiden whom the angels named Lenore—
Clasp a rare and radiant maiden, whom the angels named Lenore."
      Quoth the raven, "Nevermore."

"Be that word our sign of parting, bird or fiend!" I shrieked upstarting—
"Get thee back into the tempest and the Night's Plutonian shore!
Leave no black plume as a token of that lie thy soul hath spoken!
Leave my loneliness unbroken!—quit the bust above my door!
Take thy beak from out my heart, and take thy form from off my door!"
      Quoth the raven, "Nevermore."

And the raven, never flitting, still is sitting, still is sitting
On the pallid bust of Pallas just above my chamber door;
And his eyes have all the seeming of a demon's that is dreaming,
And the lamp-light o'er him streaming throws his shadow on the floor;
And my soul from out that shadow that lies floating on the floor
      Shall be lifted—nevermore!

TO HELEN

By
Edgar Allan Poe

Helen,[†] thy beauty is to me
　Like those Nicean barks of yore,[†]
That gently, o'er the perfumed sea,
　The weary, way-worn wanderer[†] bore
　To his own native shore.

On desperate seas long wont to roam,
　Thy hyacinth[†] hair, thy classic face,
Thy Naiad airs[†] have brought me home
　To the glory that was Greece,
　And the grandeur that was Rome.

Lo! in yon brilliant window-niche
　How statue-like I see thee stand,
The agate lamp within thy hand!
　Ah, Psyche,[†] from the regions which
　Are Holy-Land![†]

OLD IRONSIDES

By
Oliver Wendell Holmes

Oliver Wendell Holmes (1809-1894), first recognized as the author who helped preserve the famous battleship USS Constitution *for posterity, was actually a renowned medical doctor and college professor. Writing poetry was a hobby. Holmes was born in Massachusetts. He studied law at Harvard, but eventually switched to medicine. Because of his devotion to his profession, Holmes also studied modern medicine in Paris. He was one of several founders of the* Atlantic Monthly *to which he contributed. Although his poetry is considered light, it is beautifully lyrical and well constructed. Holmes died in Cambridge, Massachusetts.*

Ay, tear her tattered ensign down!
　　Long has it waved on high,
And many an eye has danced to see
　　That banner in the sky;
Beneath it rung the battle shout,
　　And burst the cannon's roar;
The meteor of the ocean air
　　Shall sweep the clouds no more!

Her deck, once red with heroes' blood,[†]
    Where knelt the vanquished foe,
When winds were hurrying o'er the flood,
    And waves were white below,
No more shall feel the victor's tread,
    Or know the conquered knee;
The harpies[†] of the shore shall pluck
    The eagle of the sea!

Oh, better that her shattered hulk
    Should sink beneath the wave!
Her thunders shook the mighty deep,
    And there should be her grave:
Nail to the mast her holy flag,
    Set every threadbare sail,
And give her to the god of storms,
    The lightning and the gale!

THE CHAMBERED NAUTILUS

By

Oliver Wendell Holmes

This is the ship of pearl, which, poets feign,
Sails the unshadowed main,—
The venturous bark that flings
On the sweet summer wind its purpled wings
In gulfs enchanted, where the Siren[†] sings,
And coral reefs lie bare,
Where the cold sea-maids rise to sun their streaming hair.
Its webs of living gauze no more unfurl;
Wrecked is the ship of pearl!
And every chambered cell,
Where its dim dreaming life was wont to dwell,
As the frail tenant shaped his growing shell,
Before thee lies revealed,--
Its irised ceiling rent, its sunless crypt unsealed!
Year after year beheld the silent toil
That spread his lustrous coil;
Still, as the spiral grew,
He left the past year's dwelling for the new,
Stole with soft step its shining archway through,
Built up its idle door,
Stretched in his last-found home, and knew the old no more.
Thanks for the heavenly message brought by thee,
Child of the wandering sea,
Cast from her lap, forlorn!
From thy dead lips a clearer note is born
Than ever Triton blew from wreathèd horn![†]
While on mine ear it rings,
Through the deep caves of thought I hear a voice that sings:—
Build thee more stately mansions, O my soul,
As the swift seasons roll!
Leave thy low-vaulted past!
Let each new temple, nobler than the last,
Shut thee from heaven with a dome more vast,
Till thou at length art free,
Leaving thine outgrown shell by life's unresting sea!

I KNEW A MAN BY SIGHT

By

Henry David Thoreau

Henry David Thoreau (1817-1862), one of the three great Romantic optimists, is recognized for presenting clearly the tenets of Romantic Transcendentalism. He was born and raised in Concord, Massachusetts, where he lived his entire life. Thoreau was educated at Harvard. He is remembered for building a small cabin and living at Walden Pond where he wrote his most impressive work, Walden. *Thoreau led an active social life with his many New England friends and colleagues. Being a proponent of freedom and liberty, he spent time in a local jail for refusing to pay taxes that would go toward supporting the Mexican War. Thoreau's essay "Civil Disobedience" relates his beliefs on the subject. Thoreau died of tuberculosis at the age of 45.*

> I knew a man by sight,
> A blameless wight,
> Who, for a year or more,
> Had daily passed my door,
> Yet converse none had had with him.
>
> I met him in a lane,
> Him and his cane,
> About three miles from home,
> Where I had chanced to roam,
> And volumes stared at him, and he at me.

In a more distant place
I glimpsed his face,
And bowed instinctively;
Starting he bowed to me,
Bowed simultaneously, and passed along.

Next, in a foreign land
I grasped his hand,
And had a social chat,
About this thing and that,
As I had known him well a thousand years.

Late in a wilderness
I shared his mess,
For he had hardships seen,
And I a wanderer been;
He was my bosom friend, and I was his.
And as, methinks, shall all,
Both great and small,
That ever lived on earth,
Early or late their birth,
Stranger and foe, one day each other know.

GETTYSBURG

By
Herman Melville

Herman Melville (1819-1891), one of the three Romantic pessimists, wrote the first great sea novel, Moby-Dick, considered one of the greatest American novels. One of eight children, Melville lived in New York City until the death of his father; then the family moved to Albany. He chose not to get a college education, but rather, sailed the seas for adventure and experience, which eventually showed up in his work. Melville's brilliance was not clearly respected until the 20th century. Although eventually published, his poetry was a mere avocation while he farmed to make a living. Melville died of a heart attack at age 72.

O Pride of the days in prime of the months
Now trebled in great renown,
When before the ark of our holy cause[†]
Fell Dagon[†] down-
Dagon foredoomed, who, armed and targed,
Never his impious heart enlarged
Beyond that hour; God walled his power,
And there the last invader charged.

He charged, and in that charge condensed
His all of hate and all of fire;
He sought to blast us in his scorn,
And wither us in his ire.

Before him went the shriek of shells-
Aerial screamings, taunts and yells;
Then the three waves in flashed advance
Surged, but were met, and back they set:
Pride was repelled by sterner pride,
And Right is a strong-hold yet.

Before our lines it seemed a beach
Which wild September gales have strown
With havoc on wreck, and dashed therewith
Pale crews unknown-
Men, arms, and steeds. The evening sun
Died on the face of each lifeless one,
And died along the winding marge of fight
And searching-parties lone.

Sloped on the hill the mounds were green,
Our centre held that place of graves,
And some still hold it in their swoon,
And over these a glory waves.
The warrior-monument, crashed in fight,[†]
Shall soar transfigured in loftier light,
A meaning ampler bear;
Soldier and priest with hymn and prayer
Have laid the stone, and every bone
Shall rest in honor there.

from SONG OF MYSELF

By
Walt Whitman

Walt Whitman (1819-1892) is known today as the "Poet of Democracy" and one of the Romantic optimists. He was reared in Long Island, New York. Whitman was an avid reader. Most of his work was in the printing or publishing business, even founding the Brooklyn Freeman, a free-soil paper. Whitman is popularly recognized for his avant-garde content, as well as making free verse an acceptable verse form. He is especially known for his cataloguing or listing, as in "I Hear America Singing." Nursing soldiers in Washington, D.C., gave him a deep respect for President Lincoln, whom he often saw walking to work. In response to the President's death, Whitman penned "O Captain, My Captain" and "When Lilacs Last in the Dooryard Bloom'd." Both poems show his enormous grief over the loss of the President. Whitman's most popular volume of poems was Leaves of Grass (1855). He died in New Jersey at the age of 82 after several years of poor health.

1.
I celebrate myself, and sing myself,
And what I assume you shall assume,
For every atom belonging to me as good belongs to you.

I loafe and invite my soul,
I lean and loafe at my ease observing a spear of summer grass.

My tongue, every atom of my blood, form'd from this soil, this air,
Born here of parents born here from parents the same, and their parents
          the same,
I, now thirty-seven years old in perfect health begin,
Hoping to cease not till death.

Creeds and schools in abeyance,
Retiring back a while sufficed at what they are, but never forgotten,
I harbor for good or bad, I permit to speak at every hazard,
Nature without check with original energy.

2.

Houses and rooms are full of perfumes, the shelves are crowded with
          perfumes,
I breathe the fragrance myself and know it and like it,
The distillation would intoxicate me also, but I shall not let it.

The atmosphere is not a perfume, it has no taste of the distillation, it is
          odorless,
It is for my mouth forever, I am in love with it,
I will go to the bank by the wood and become undisguised and naked,
I am mad for it to be in contact with me.

The smoke of my own breath,
Echoes, ripples, buzz'd whispers, love-root, silk-thread, crotch and vine,
My respiration and inspiration, the beating of my heart, the passing of
          blood and air through my lungs,
The sniff of green leaves and dry leaves, and of the shore and dark-color'd
          sea-rocks, and of hay in the barn,

The sound of the belch'd words of my voice loos'd to the eddies of the
          wind,
A few light kisses, a few embraces, a reaching around of arms,
The play of shine and shade on the trees as the supple boughs wag,
The delight alone or in the rush of the streets, or along the fields and
          hill-sides,
The feeling of health, the full-noon trill, the song of me rising from bed
          and meeting the sun.

Have you reckon'd a thousand acres much? have you reckon'd the earth
    much?
Have you practis'd so long to learn to read?
Have you felt so proud to get at the meaning of poems?

Stop this day and night with me and you shall possess the origin of all
    poems,
You shall possess the good of the earth and sun, (there are millions of suns
    left,)
You shall no longer take things at second or third hand, nor look through
    the eyes of the dead, nor feed on the spectres in books,
You shall not look through my eyes either, nor take things from me,
You shall listen to all sides and filter them from your self.

3.

I have heard what the talkers were talking, the talk of the beginning and
    the end,
But I do not talk of the beginning or the end.

There was never any more inception than there is now,
Nor any more youth or age than there is now,
And will never be any more perfection than there is now,
Nor any more heaven or hell than there is now.

Urge and urge and urge,
Always the procreant urge of the world.

Out of the dimness opposite equals advance, always substance and
    increase, always sex,
Always a knit of identity, always distinction, always a breed of life.

To elaborate is no avail, learn'd and unlearn'd feel that it is so.

Sure as the most certain sure, plumb in the uprights,[†] well entretied,
    braced in the beams,
Stout as a horse, affectionate, haughty, electrical,
I and this mystery here we stand.

Clear and sweet is my soul, and clear and sweet is all that is not my soul.

Lack one lacks both, and the unseen is proved by the seen,
Till that becomes unseen and receives proof in its turn.
Showing the best and dividing it from the worst age vexes age,
Knowing the perfect fitness and equanimity of things, while they discuss I
      am silent, and go bathe and admire myself.
Welcome is every organ and attribute of me, and of any man hearty and
      clean,
Not an inch nor a particle of an inch is vile, and none shall be less familiar
      than the rest.

I am satisfied—I see, dance, laugh, sing;
As the hugging and loving bed-fellow sleeps at my side through the night,
      and withdraws at the peep of the day with stealthy tread,
Leaving me baskets cover'd with white towels swelling the house with
      their plenty,
Shall I postpone my acceptation and realization and scream at my eyes,
That they turn from gazing after and down the road,
And forthwith cipher and show me to a cent,
Exactly the value of one and exactly the value of two, and which is ahead?

4.

Trippers and askers surround me,
People I meet, the effect upon me of my early life or the ward and city I
      live in, or the nation,
The latest dates, discoveries, inventions, societies, authors old and new,
My dinner, dress, associates, looks, compliments, dues,
The real or fancied indifference of some man or woman I love,
The sickness of one of my folks or of myself, or ill-doing or loss or lack of
      money, or depressions or exaltations,
Battles, the horrors of fratricidal war, the fever of doubtful news, the fitful
      events;
These come to me days and nights and go from me again,
But they are not the Me myself.

Apart from the pulling and hauling stands what I am,
Stands amused, complacent, compassionating, idle, unitary,
Looks down, is erect, or bends an arm on an impalpable certain rest,
Looking with side-curved head curious what will come next,
Both in and out of the game and watching and wondering at it.

Backward I see in my own days where I sweated through fog with linguists
　　and contenders,
I have no mockings or arguments, I witness and wait.

5.

I believe in you my soul, the other I am must not abase itself to you,
And you must not be abased to the other.
Loafe with me on the grass, loose the stop from your throat,
Not words, not music or rhyme I want, not custom or lecture, not even the
　　best,
Only the lull I like, the hum of your valved voice.

I mind how once we lay such a transparent summer morning,
How you settled your head athwart my hips and gently turn'd over upon
　　me,
And parted the shirt from my bosom-bone, and plunged your tongue to
　　my bare-stript heart,
And reach'd till you felt my beard, and reach'd till you held my feet.

Swiftly arose and spread around me the peace and knowledge that pass all
　　the argument of the earth,
And I know that the hand of God is the promise of my own,
And I know that the spirit of God is the brother of my own,
And that all the men ever born are also my brothers, and the women my
　　sisters and lovers,
And that a kelson of the creation is love,
And limitless are leaves stiff or drooping in the fields,
And brown ants in the little wells beneath them,
And mossy scabs of the worm fence, heap'd stones, elder, mullein and
　　poke-weed.

6.

A child said What is the grass? fetching it to me with full hands;
How could I answer the child? I do not know what it is any more than he.

I guess it must be the flag of my disposition, out of hopeful green stuff
　　woven.

Or I guess it is the handkerchief of the Lord,
A scented gift and remembrancer designedly dropt,
Bearing the owner's name someway in the corners, that we may see and
　　remark, and say Whose?

Or I guess the grass is itself a child, the produced babe of the vegetation.

Or I guess it is a uniform hieroglyphic,
And it means, Sprouting alike in broad zones and narrow zones,
Growing among black folks as among white,
Kanuck,[†] Tuckahoe,[†] Congressman, Cuff,[†] I give them the same, I receive
     them the same.
And now it seems to me the beautiful uncut hair of graves.

Tenderly will I use you curling grass,
It may be you transpire from the breasts of young men,
It may be if I had known them I would have loved them,
It may be you are from old people, or from offspring taken soon out of
          their mothers' laps,
And here you are the mothers' laps.

This grass is very dark to be from the white heads of old mothers,
Darker than the colorless beards of old men,
Dark to come from under the faint red roofs of mouths.
O I perceive after all so many uttering tongues,
And I perceive they do not come from the roofs of mouths for nothing.

I wish I could translate the hints about the dead young men and women,
And the hints about old men and mothers, and the offspring taken soon
          out of their laps.

What do you think has become of the young and old men?
And what do you think has become of the women and children?

They are alive and well somewhere,
The smallest sprout shows there is really no death,
And if ever there was it led forward life, and does not wait at the end to
          arrest it,

And ceas'd the moment life appear'd.
All goes onward and outward, nothing collapses,
And to die is different from what any one supposed, and luckier.

7.
Has any one supposed it lucky to be born?
I hasten to inform him or her it is just as lucky to die, and I know it.

I pass death with the dying and birth with the new-wash'd babe, and am
    not contain'd between my hat and boots,
And peruse manifold objects, no two alike and every one good,
The earth good and the stars good, and their adjuncts all good.

I am not an earth nor an adjunct of an earth,
I am the mate and companion of people, all just as immortal and fathom
    less as myself,
(They do not know how immortal, but I know.)

Every kind for itself and its own, for me mine male and female,
For me those that have been boys and that love women,
For me the man that is proud and feels how it stings to be slighted,
For me the sweet-heart and the old maid, for me mothers and the mothers
    of mothers,
For me lips that have smiled, eyes that have shed tears,
For me children and the begetters of children.

Undrape! you are not guilty to me, nor stale nor discarded,
I see through the broadcloth and gingham whether or no,
And am around, tenacious, acquisitive, tireless, and cannot be shaken
    away.

I HEAR AMERICA SINGING

By
Walt Whitman

I HEAR America singing, the varied carols I hear,
Those of mechanics, each one singing his, as it should be, blithe and
      strong,
The carpenter singing his as he measures his plank or beam,
The mason singing his as he makes ready for work, or leaves off work,
The boatman singing what belongs to him in his boat, the deckhand
      singing on the steamboat deck,
The shoemaker singing as he sits on his bench, the hatter singing as he
      stands,
The wood-cutter's song, the ploughboy's, on his way in the morning, or at
      the noon intermission, or at sundown,
The delicious singing of the mother, or of the young wife at work, or of the
      girl sewing or washing,
Each singing what belongs to her, and to none else,
The day what belongs to the day—at night, the party of young fellows,
      robust, friendly,
Singing, with open mouths, their strong melodious songs.

O Captain! My Captain!

By
Walt Whitman

O Captain![†] my Captain! our fearful trip is done,
The ship[†] has weather'd every rack, the prize we sought is won,
The port is near, the bells I hear, the people all exulting,
While follow eyes the steady keel, the vessel grim and daring;
  But O heart! heart! heart!
    O the bleeding drops of red,
      Where on the deck my Captain lies,
        Fallen cold and dead.

O Captain! my Captain! rise up and hear the bells;
Rise up—for you the flag is flung—for you the bugle trills,
For you bouquets and ribbon'd wreaths—for you the shores a-crowding;
For you they call, the swaying mass, their eager faces turning;
  Here Captain! dear father!
    This arm beneath your head!
      It is some dream that on the deck,
        You've fallen cold and dead.

My Captain does not answer, his lips are pale and still,
My father does not feel my arm, he has no pulse nor will,
The ship is anchor'd safe and sound, its voyage closed and done,
From fearful trip, the victor ship comes in with object won;
  Exult, O shores, and ring O bells!
    But I with mournful tread,
      Walk the deck my Captain lies,
        Fallen cold and dead.

WHEN I HEARD THE LEARN'D ASTRONOMER

By
Walt Whitman

When I heard the learn'd astronomer,
When the proofs, the figures, were ranged in columns before me,
When I was shown the charts, the diagrams, to add, divide, and measure
      them,
When I sitting heard the astronomer where he lectured with much
      applause in the lecture room,
How soon unaccountable I became tired and sick,
Till rising and gliding out I wander'd off by myself,
In the mystical moist night-air, and from time to time,
Look'd up in perfect silence at the stars.

THE BATTLE HYMN OF THE REPUBLIC

By
Julia Ward Howe

Julia Ward Howe (1819-1910), an abolitionist and suffragette, was an early proponent for social justice. Coming from a wealthy New York family, she was educated, particularly in languages and music. Howe enjoyed the luxury and society of a prominent family. In her day, she was a recognized social force, but today she is remembered for her poem, "The Battle Hymn of the Republic," which became the battle song of the North during the Civil War. At age 91, Julia Ward Howe died of pneumonia at home in Portsmouth, Rhode Island

Mine eyes have seen the glory of the coming of the Lord:
He is trampling out the vintage where the grapes of wrath are stored;
He hath loosed the fateful lightning of His terrible swift sword:
    His truth is marching on.

I have seen Him in the watch-fires of a hundred circling camps;
They have builded Him an altar in the evening dews and damps;
I can read His righteous sentence by the dim and flaring lamps.
    His day is marching on.

I have read a fiery gospel, writ in burnished rows of steel:
"As ye deal with my contemners, so with you my grace shall deal;
Let the Hero, born of woman, crush the serpent with his heel,[†]
    Since God is marching on."

He has sounded forth the trumpet that shall never call retreat;
He is sifting out the hearts of men before His judgment seat:
Oh! be swift, my soul, to answer Him! be jubilant, my feet!
    Our God is marching on.

In the beauty of the lilies Christ was born across the sea,
With a glory in His bosom that transfigures you and me:
As He died to make men holy, let us die to make men free,
    While God is marching on.

BECAUSE I COULD NOT STOP FOR DEATH

By

Emily Dickinson

Emily Dickinson (1830-1886) lived almost her entire life in Amherst, Massachusetts. She was quite reclusive and seldom left her house; in fact, she is buried within sight of her home. Between 1862 and 1863, Dickinson wrote nearly one poem a day, but none deals with the Civil War. Instead, her poetry reflects her loneliness and a general state of longing, coupled with some inspirational moments that suggest the possibility of happiness. Only seven of her 1,775 poems were published during her lifetime, and these were substantively altered without her permission. Her poems, consisting primarily of short stanzas, frequently deal with death and the effects of time. Modern critics consider Dickinson a uniquely American poetic voice, whose poems rose above the limits imposed upon her by both her gender and the time in which she lived.

> Because I could not stop for Death,
> He kindly stopped for me;
> The carriage held but just ourselves
> And Immortality.
>
> We slowly drove, he knew no haste,
> And I had put away
> My labor, and my leisure too,
> For his civility.

We passed the school, where children played
Their lessons scarcely done;
We passed the fields of gazing grain,
We passed the setting sun.

We paused before house that seemed
A swelling of the ground;
The roof was scarcely visible,
The cornice but a mound.

Since then 'tis centuries; but each
Feels shorter than the day
I first surmised the horses' heads
Were toward eternity.

HOPE IS THE THING WITH FEATHERS

By
Emily Dickinson

Hope is the thing with feathers
That perches in the soul,
And sings the tune without the words,
And never stops at all,

And sweetest in the gale is heard;
And sore must be the storm
That could abash the little bird
That kept so many warm.

I've heard it in the chillest land,
And on the strangest sea;
Yet, never, in extremity,
It asked a crumb of me.

I CAN WADE GRIEF

By
Emily Dickinson

I can wade Grief—
Whole Pools of it—
I'm used to that—
But the least push of Joy
Breaks up my feet—
And I tip—drunken—
Let no Pebble—smile—
'Twas the New Liquor—
That was all!

Power is only Pain—
Stranded, thro' Discipline,
Till Weights—will hang—
Give Balm—to Giants—
And they'll wilt, like Men—
Give Himmaleh†—
They'll carry—Him!

I DIED FOR BEAUTY

By
Emily Dickinson

I died for beauty, but was scarce
Adjusted in the tomb,
When one who died for truth was lain
In an adjoining room.

He questioned softly why I failed?
"For beauty," I replied.
"And I for truth,—the two are one;
We brethren are," he said.

And so, as kinsmen met a night,
We talked between the rooms,
Until the moss had reached our lips,
And covered up our names.

I HEARD A FLY BUZZ WHEN I DIED

By
Emily Dickinson

I heard a fly buzz when I died;
    The stillness round my form
Was like the stillness in the air
    Between the heaves of storm.

The eyes beside had wrung them dry,
    And breaths were gathering sure
For that last onset, when the king[†]
    Be witnessed in his power.

I willed my keepsakes, signed away
    What portion of me I
Could make assignable,—and then
    There interposed a fly,

With blue, uncertain, stumbling buzz,
    Between the light and me;
And then the windows[†] failed, and then
    I could not see to see.

I NEVER SAW A MOOR

By
Emily Dickinson

I never saw a moor,
I never saw the sea;
Yet know I how the heather looks,
And what a wave must be.

I never spoke with God,
Nor visited in heaven;
Yet certain am I of the spot
As if the chart were given.

I'M NOBODY!
WHO ARE YOU?

By
Emily Dickinson

I'm nobody! Who are you?
Are you nobody, too?
Then there's a pair of us—don't tell!
They'd banish us, you know.

How dreary to be somebody!
How public, like a frog
To tell your name the livelong day
To an admiring bog!

SUCCESS IS COUNTED SWEETEST

By
Emily Dickinson

Success is counted sweetest
By those who ne'er succeed.
To comprehend a nectar
Requires sorest need.

Not one of all the purple host
Who took the flag to-day
Can tell the definition,
So clear, of victory,

As he, defeated, dying,
On whose forbidden ear
The distant strains of triumph
Burst agonized and clear!

ROMEO AND JULIET

By
Thomas Bailey Aldrich

Thomas Bailey Aldrich (1836-1907), born in Portsmouth, New Hampshire, but raised in New Orleans, decided to become a poet after reading the works of several great American poets. Although he had no formal college education, Aldrich became a businessman and eventually a writer for and editor of popular magazines, such as the Atlantic Monthly. *As a young man, Aldrich published his works in magazines. In his poetry, he was able to present a single incident in a moving and expressive manner. Aldrich died in Boston at the age of 71.*

From mask to mask, amid the masquerade,
Young Passion went with challenging, soft breath:
Art Love? he whispered; art thou Love, sweet maid?
Then Love, with glittering eyelids, I am Death.

A Morning Fancy

By
Ambrose Bierce

Ambrose Bierce (1842-c.1914) was born in Ohio, but grew up in Indiana. He served in the Union infantry during the Civil War and fought in the Battle of Shiloh, which influenced much of his later writing and, undoubtedly, influenced his outlook on war and humanity in general. Bierce worked for newspapers in San Francisco, becoming a famous columnist and influential editor. His works are filled with social satire, ridicule, and wit. After sending a letter to a friend on December 26, 1913, he vanished while traveling as an observer of the Mexican Revolution with Pancho Villa's army.

Drifted (or I seemed to) in a boat
Upon the surface of a shoreless sea
Whereon no ship nor anything did float,
Save only the frail bark supporting me;
And that—it was so shadowy—seemed to be
Almost from out the subtle azure wrought
Of the great ocean underneath its keel;
And all that blue profound appeared as naught
But thicker sky, translucent to reveal,
Miles down, whatever through its spaces glided,
Or at the bottom traveled or abided.

Great cities there I saw; of rich and poor
The palace and the hovel; mountains, vales,
Forest and field; the desert and the moor;
Tombs of the good and wise who'd lived in jails;
Seas of a denser fluid, white with sails
Pushed at by currents moving here and there
And sensible to sight above the flat
Of that opaquer deep. Ah, strange and fair
The nether world that I was gazing at
With beating heart from that exalted level,
And, lest I founder, trembling like the devil!

The cities all were populous: men swarmed
In public places—chattered, laughed and wept;
And savages their shining bodies warmed
At fires in primal woods. The wild beast leapt
Upon its prey and slew it as it slept.
Armies went forth to battle on the plain
So far, far down in that unfathomed deep
The living seemed as silent as the slain,
Nor even the windows could be heard to weep.
One might have thought their shaking was but laughter;
And, truly, most were married shortly after.

Above the wreckage of that silent fray
Strange fishes swam in circles, round and round—
Black, double-finned; and once a little way
A bubble rose and burst without a sound
And a man tumbled out upon the ground.
Lord! 'twas an eerie thing to drift apace
On that pellucid sea, beneath black skies
And o'er the heads of an undrowning race!
And when I woke I said—to her surprise
Who came with chocolate, for me to drink it:
"The atmosphere is deeper than you think it."

THE NEW COLOSSUS †

By

Emma Lazarus

Emma Lazarus (1849-1887) was a writer whose pinnacle of success was when her sonnet, "The New Colossus" (1983), was placed at the foot of the Statue of Liberty in 1912. Lazarus was born in New York to wealthy Jewish parents. Because of the family's prosperity and her father's indulgence, she was privately tutored, especially in languages, and then was able to spend her life writing. Her Jewish background and love of America infused her works. Besides poetry, Lazarus wrote two plays and a novel, as well as translating Italian and German poetry. She died of Hodgkin's disease when she was only 38.

Not like the brazen giant of Greek fame,†
With conquering limbs astride from land to land;
Here at our sea-washed, sunset gates shall stand
A mighty woman with a torch,† whose flame
Is the imprisoned lightning, and her name
Mother of Exiles. From her beacon-hand
Glows world-wide welcome; her mild eyes command
The air-bridged harbor that twin cities frame.†
"Keep, ancient lands,† your storied pomp!†" cries she
With silent lips. "Give me your tired, your poor,
Your huddled masses yearning to breathe free,
The wretched refuse of your teeming shore.
Send these, the homeless, tempest-tost to me,
I lift my lamp beside the golden door!†"

A CAGED BIRD

By
Sarah Orne Jewett

Sarah Orne Jewett (1849-1909) was an outstanding regionalist writer of the late 19th century. Her writing often focuses on character and appealing descriptions of her home state of Maine. Because of childhood arthritis, Jewett spent many hours traveling with her physician father as he visited his patients. Jewett did not go to college, but she educated herself by reading extensively. Her first published work was in the Atlantic Monthly *when she was only 19 years old. Developing her natural talents, Jewett became an important New England writer. She was the first woman to receive an honorary doctorate from Bowdoin College. Jewett barely wrote after being badly injured in a carriage accident. She died of a stroke at her home in 1909.*

High at the window in her cage,
    The old canary sits and sings,
Nor sees across the curtain pass
    The shadow of a swallow's wings.

A poor deceit and copy, this,
    Of larger lives that count their span,
Unreckoning of wider worlds,
    Or gifts that Heaven keeps for man.

She gathers piteous bits and shreds,
    This solitary, mateless thing,

Patient to build again the nest
    So rudely scattered spring by spring;

And sings her brief, unlistened songs,
    Her dreams of bird life wild and free,
Yet never beats her prison bars
    At sound of song from bush or tree.

Yet in my busiest hours I pause,
    Held by a sense of urgent speech,
Bewildered by that spark-like soul,
    Able my very soul to reach.

She will be heard; she chirps me loud,
    When I forget those gravest cares,
Her small provision to supply,
    Clear water or the seedsman's wares.

She begs me now for that chief joy
    The round great world is made to grow,—
Her wisp of greenness. Hear her chide,
    Because my answering thought is slow!

What can my life seem like to her?
    A dull, unpunctual service mine;
Stupid before her eager call,
    Her flitting steps, her insight fine!

To open wide thy prison door,
    Poor friend, would give thee to thy foes;
And yet a plaintive note I hear,
    As if to tell how slowly goes

The time of thy long prisoning.
    Bird! does some promise keep thee sane?
Will there be better days for thee?
    Will thy soul too know life again?

Ah, none of us have more than this:
    If one true friend green leaves can reach
From out some fairer, wider place,
    And understand our wistful speech!

THE BUMBLEBEE

By

James Whitcomb Riley

James Whitcomb Riley (1849-1916), often called the "Hoosier Poet," was a popular mid-western poet from Greenfield, Indiana. Unlike many other poets, Riley did not complete high school. His love of the land and lifestyle of the mid-west and the local dialects fill his poems. Riley's works have great appeal because of their folksy tone and emphasis on the positive aspects of rural life. He was greatly loved and extremely popular in his day. Besides his volumes of poetry, Riley was known for his vibrant oral presentations. He died at age 66 of a stroke

> You better not fool with a Bumblebee!—
> Ef you don't think they can sting—you'll see!
> They're lazy to look at, an' kind o' go
> Buzzin' an' bummin' aroun' so slow,
> An' ac' so slouchy an' all fagged out,[†]
> Danglin' their legs as they drone about
> The hollyhawks[†] 'at they can't climb in
> 'Ithout ist a-tumble-un out ag'in!
> Wunst I watched one climb clean 'way
> In a jimson-blossom,[†] I did, one day,—
> An' I ist grabbed it—an' nen let go—
> An' "Ooh-ooh! Honey! I told ye so!"
> Says The Raggedy Man;[†] an' he ist run

An' pullt out the stinger, an' don't laugh none,
An' says: "They has be'n folks, I guess,
'At thought I wuz predjudust, more er less,—
Yit I still muntain[†] 'at a Bumblebee
Wears out his welcome too quick fer me!"

WHEN THE FROST IS ON THE PUNKIN

By

James Whitcomb Riley

When the frost is on the punkin and the fodder's[†] in the shock,[†]
And you hear the kyouck and gobble of the struttin' turkey-cock
And the clackin' of the guineys, and the cluckin'[†] of the hens,
And the rooster's hallylooyer as he tiptoes on the fence;
O, it's then's the times a feller is a-feelin' at his best,
With the risin' sun to greet him from a night of peaceful rest,
As he leaves the house, bareheaded, and goes out to feed the stock,
When the frost is on the punkin and the fodder's in the shock.

They's something kindo' harty-like about the atmusfere
When the heat of summer's over and the coolin' fall is here—
Of course we miss the flowers, and the blossums on the trees,
And the mumble of the hummin'-birds and buzzin' of the bees;
But the air's so appetizin'; and the landscape through the haze
Of a crisp and sunny morning of the airly[†] autumn days
Is a pictur' that no painter has the colorin' to mock—
When the frost is on the punkin and the fodder's in the shock.

The husky, rusty russel of the tossels of the corn,[†]
And the raspin' of the tangled leaves, as golden as the morn;
The stubble in the furries[†]—kindo' lonesome-like, but still
A-preachin' sermuns to us of the barns they growed to fill;
The strawstack in the medder,[†] and the reaper in the shed;
The hosses[†] in theyr stalls below—the clover over-head![†]—
O, it sets my hart a-clickin' like the tickin' of a clock,
When the frost is on the punkin and the fodder's in the shock!

Then your apples all is gethered, and the ones a feller keeps
Is poured around the celler-floor[†] in red and yeller heaps;
And your cider-makin' 's over, and your wimmern-folks is through
With their mince and apple-butter, and theyr souse and saussage,[†] too!
I don't know how to tell it—but ef sich a thing could be
As the Angels wantin' boardin', and they'd call around on me—
I'd want to 'commodate 'em—all the whole-indurin' flock—
When the frost is on the punkin and the fodder's in the shock!

SOLITUDE

By
Ella Wheeler Wilcox

Ella Wheeler Wilcox (1850-1919) in her lifetime was a popular and outstanding poet of the common individual. She had a wide audience who read her verses in the newspaper. Born in Johnstown, Wisconsin, Wilcox was not college educated, but was fortunate in coming from a home of poets and readers. The philosophy she espoused was called New Thought, but she added her own ideas from Spiritualism. Her poetry was not regarded highly by critics or poets; however, two lines of "Solitude" are two of the most remembered lines in poetry. Wilcox died at her home in Short Beach, Connecticut.

> Laugh, and the world laughs with you;
>   Weep, and you weep alone.
> For the sad old earth must borrow its mirth,
>   But has trouble enough of its own.
> Sing, and the hills will answer;
>   Sigh, it is lost on the air.
> The echoes bound to a joyful sound,
>   But shrink from voicing care.
>
> Rejoice, and men will seek you;
>   Grieve, and they turn and go.
> They want full measure of all your pleasure,
>   Bit they do not need your woe.
> Be glad, and your friends are many;

Be sad, and you lose them all.
There are none to decline your nectared wine,
    But alone you must drink life's gall.

Feast, and your halls are crowded;
    Fast, and the world goes by.
Succeed and give, and it helps you live,
    But no man can help you die.
There is room in the halls of pleasure
    For a long and lordly train,
But one by one we must all file on
    Through the narrow aisles of pain.

IN WAR-TIME
(AN AMERICAN
HOMEWARD-BOUND)

By

Florence Earle Coates

Florence Earle Coates (1850-1927) was born in Philadelphia and educated at private schools there, as well as in France and Brussels. She authored only 39 poems, and these were written between the years of 1888-1919. Most of her poetry was published in magazines, and she played a prominent role in Philadelphia's literary life. In 1879, she married Edward Coates, who served as President of the Philadelphia Academy of Fine Arts. Much of her work deals with quiet aspects of nature and elements of war, primarily focusing on how individual bravery reflects patriotism.

Further and further we leave the scene
Of war—and of England's care;
I try to keep my mind serene—
But my heart stays there;
For a distant song of pain and wrong
My spirit doth deep confuse,
And I sit all day on the deck, and long—
And long for news!
I seem to see them in battle-line—

Heroes with hearts of gold,
But of their victory a sign
The Fates[†] withhold;
And the hours too tardy-footed pass,
The voiceless hush grows dense
'Mid the imaginings, alas!
That feed suspense.
Oh, might I lie on the wind, or fly
In the wilful sea-bird's track,
Would I hurry on, with a homesick cry—
Or hasten back?

TEARS

By

Lizette Woodworth Reese

Lizette Woodworth Reese (1856-1935) was a public school teacher in Maryland for 45 years, as well as a poet. Her first published work was in 1874 in Baltimore's Southern Magazine. *H.L. Mencken, a popular editor, praised her work; in fact Emily Dickinson and Reese are often considered similar in their work. Reese received several awards, including Poet Laureate of the General Federation of Women (1931), and an honorary Doctorate from Goucher College. She died in Baltimore, Maryland.*

When I consider Life and its few years—
A wisp of fog betwixt us and the sun;
A call to battle, and the battle done
Ere the last echo dies within our ears;
A rose choked in the grass; an hour of fears;
The gusts that past a darkening shore do beat;
The burst of music down an unlistening street—
I wonder at the idleness of tears.
Ye old, old dead, and ye of yesternight,
Chieftains, and bards, and keepers of the sheep,
By every cup of sorrow that you had,
Loose me from tears, and make me see aright
How each hath back at once he stayed to weep:
Homer his sight,[†] David his little lad![†]

AMERICA THE BEAUTIFUL

By

Katherine Lee Bates

Katherine Lee Bates (1859-1929), born in Falmouth, Massachusetts, was another versatile writer of poetry and prose from New England. She wrote children's stories and works about Shakespeare. After attending Wellesley College, Bates became a professor of literature at her alma mater. While on one of her many excursions, she visited the American West. Overwhelmed by the various sights, especially on the top of Pike's Peak, she wrote her beloved "America the Beautiful" (1895), a song often recommended to replace the current National Anthem. Bates was 69 when she died in Wellesley, Massachusetts.

O beautiful for spacious skies,
　For amber waves of grain,[†]
For purple mountain majesties
　Above the fruited plain!
　　America! America!
　God shed his grace on thee
And crown thy good with brotherhood
　From sea to shining sea![†]

O beautiful for pilgrim feet,
　Whose stern impassioned stress
A thoroughfare of freedom beat
　Across the wilderness!

America! America!
God mend thine every flaw,
Confirm thy soul in self-control,
   Thy liberty in law!

O beautiful for heroes proved
   In liberating strife,
Who more than self their country loved,
   And mercy more than life!
      America! America!
May God thy gold refine,
Till all success be nobleness,
   And every gain divine!

O beautiful for patriot dream
   That sees beyond the years
Thine alabaster cities gleam
   Undimmed by human tears!
      America! America!
God shed his grace on thee
And crown thy good with brotherhood
   From sea to shining sea!

CASEY AT THE BAT

By
Ernest Thayer

Ernest Thayer (1863-1940) was little known as a poet in his day. Raised in Massachusetts and educated at Harvard, Thayer was a humorous writer for Hearst's newspaper, where he also published some poetry. Using the pen name "Phin," he published "Casey at the Bat," which appeared in 1888, in the Examiner. The poem's fame came when recited before the August 1888 Chicago Cubs (then the White Stockings) and New York Giants game. A cerebral hemorrhage claimed Thayer's life when he was 77 years old.

It looked extremely rocky for the Mudville nine that day;
The score stood four to two, with but one inning more to play.
And then when Cooney died at first, and Barrows did the same,
A sickly silence fell upon the patrons of the game.

A straggling few got up to go, leaving there the rest,
With the hope which springs eternal in the human breast. [†]
They thought: "If only Casey could get but a whack at that,"
They'd put even money, now, with Casey at the bat.

But Flynn preceded Casey, and likewise so did Blake,
And the former was a pudd'n, and the latter was a fake.
So on that stricken multitude a deathlike silence sat;
For there seemed but little chance of Casey's getting to the bat.

But Flynn let drive a "single," to the wonderment of all.
And the much-despised Blakey "tore the cover off the ball."
And when the dust had lifted, and they saw what had occurred,
There was Blakey safe at second, and Flynn a-huggin' third.

Then from the gladdened multitude went up a joyous yell—
It rumbled in the mountaintops, it rattled in the dell;
It struck upon the hillside and rebounded on the flat;
For Casey, mighty Casey, was advancing to the bat.

There was ease in Casey's manner as he stepped into his place,
There was pride in Casey's bearing and a smile on Casey's face;
And when responding to the cheers he lightly doffed his hat,
No stranger in the crowd could doubt 'twas Casey at the bat.

Ten thousand eyes were on him as he rubbed his hands with dirt,
Five thousand tongues applauded when he wiped them on his shirt;
Then when the writhing pitcher ground the ball into his hip,
Defiance glanced in Casey's eye, a sneer curled Casey's lip.

And now the leather-covered sphere came hurtling through the air,
And Casey stood a watching it in haughty grandeur there.
Close by the sturdy batsman the ball unheeded sped;
"That ain't my style," said Casey. "Strike one," the umpire said.

From the benches, black with people, there went up a muffled roar,
Like the beating of the storm waves on the stern and distant shore.
"Kill him! kill the umpire!" shouted someone on the stand;
And it's likely they'd have killed him had not Casey raised his hand.

With a smile of Christian charity great Casey's visage shone;
He stilled the rising tumault, he made the game go on;
He signaled to the pitcher, and once more the spheroid flew;
But Casey still ignored it, and the umpire said, "Strike two."

"Fraud!" cried the maddened thousands, and the echo answered "Fraud!"
But one scornful look from Casey and the audience was awed;
They saw his face grow stern and cold, they saw his muscles strain,
And they knew that Casey wouldn't let the ball go by again.

The sneer is gone from Casey's lips, his teeth are clenched in hate,
He pounds with cruel violence his bat upon the plate;

And now the pitcher holds the ball, and now he lets it go,
And now the air is shattered by the force of Casey's blow.

Oh, somewhere in this favored land the sun is shining bright,
The band is playing somewhere, and somewhere hearts are light;
And somewhere men are laughing, and somewhere children shout,
But there is no joy in Mudville: Mighty Casey has struck out.

WHEN OL' SIS' JUDY PRAY

By

James Edwin Campbell

James Edwin Campbell (1867-1896) was an American poet, editor, short story writer, and educator. He was born in Pomeroy, Ohio, and died there in 1896. Campbell attended Miami College of Ohio and wrote regularly for daily news-papers in Chicago during the 1880s and 1890s. He was also President of West Virginia Colored Institute, which is now West Virginia State College. Campbell's poems are written in the dialect he was exposed to in his early years, as well as in Standard English.

WHEN ol' Sis' Judy pray,
De teahs come stealin' down my cheek,
De voice ur God widin me speak';
I see myse'f so po' an' weak,
Down on my knees de cross I seek,
When ol' Sis' Judy pray.

When ol' Sis' Judy pray,
De thun'ers ur Mount Sin-a-i[†]
Comes rushin' down f'um up on high—
De Debbil tu'n[†] his back an' fly
While sinnahs[†] loud fur pa'don cry,
When ol' Sis' Judy pray.

 When ol' Sis' Judy pray,
Ha'd sinnahs trimble in dey seat
Ter hyuh huh voice in sorro 'peat[†]
(While all de chu'ch des sob an' weep)
"O Shepa'd, dese, dy po' los' sheep!"
When ol' Sis' Judy pray.

When ol' Sis' Judy pray,
De whole house hit des rock an' moan
Ter see huh teahs an' hyuh huh groan;
Dar's somepin' in Sis' Judy's tone
Dat melt all ha'ts dough med ur stone[†]
When ol' Sis' Judy pray.

When ol' Sis' Judy pray,
Salvation's light comes pourin' down—
Hit fill de chu'ch an' all de town—
Why, angels' robes go rustlin' 'roun',
An' hebben on de Yurf am foun',[†]
When ol' Sis' Judy pray.

When ol' Sis' Judy pray,
My soul go sweepin' up on wings,
An' loud de chu'ch wid "Glory!" rings,
An' wide de gates ur Jahsper[†] swings
Twel you hyuh ha'ps wid golding strings,
When ol' Sis' Judy pray.

ANER CLUTE

By

Edgar Lee Masters

Edgar Lee Masters (1868-1950) is an author whose reputation rests mainly on one work, Spoon River Anthology (1915). Born in Garnett, Kansas, he spent his childhood in western Illinois; at that time, it was mostly unsettled farmland. Although not a college graduate, Masters was an avid reader and, eventually, a lawyer. His various works show his ambivalence about small town living and farm life. Spoon River Anthology is an intriguing work of 244 short, free verse monologues, spoken by dead inhabitants of Spoon River, presenting the happiness as well as the despair of their lives. At 72 years old, Masters died in Philadelphia.

Over and over they used to ask me,
While buying the wine or the beer,
In Peoria first, and later in Chicago,
Denver, Frisco, New York, wherever I lived,
How I happened to lead the life,
And what was the start of it.
Well, I told them a silk dress,
And a promise of marriage from a rich man—
(It was Lucius Atherton).
But that was not really it at all.
Suppose a boy steals an apple
From the tray at the grocery store,

And they all begin to call him a thief,
The editor, minister, judge, and all the people—
"A thief," "a thief," "a thief," wherever he goes.
And he can't get work, and he can't get bread
Without stealing it, why, the boy will steal.
It's the way the people regard the theft of the apple
That makes the boy what he is.

HOD PUTT

By
Edgar Lee Masters

Here I lie close to the grave
Of Old Bill Piersol,
Who grew rich trading with the Indians, and who
Afterwards took the bankrupt law
And emerged from it richer than ever.
Myself grown tired of toil and poverty
And beholding how Old Bill and others grew in wealth,
Robbed a traveler one night near Proctor's Grove,
Killing him unwittingly while doing so,
For the which I was tried and hanged.
That was my way of going into bankruptcy.
Now we who took the bankrupt law in our respective ways
Sleep peacefully side by side.

HOMER CLAPP

By
Edgar Lee Masters

Often Aner Clute at the gate
Refused me the parting kiss,
Saying we should be engaged before that;
And just with a distant clasp of the hand
She bade me good-night, as I brought her home
From the skating rink or the revival.
No sooner did my departing footsteps die away
Than Lucius Atherton,
(So I learned when Aner went to Peoria)
Stole in at her window, or took her riding
Behind his spanking team of bays
Into the country.
The shock of it made me settle down,
And I put all the money I got from my father's estate
Into the canning factory, to get the job
Of head accountant, and lost it all.
And then I knew I was one of Life's fools,
Whom only death would treat as the equal
Of other men, making me feel like a man.

THE HILL

By
Edgar Lee Masters

Where are Elmer, Herman, Bert, Tom, and Charley,
The weak of will, the strong of arm, the clown, the boozer, the fighter?
All, all, are sleeping on the hill.[†]

One passed in a fever,
One was burned in a mine,
One was killed in a brawl,
One died in jail,
One fell from a bridge toiling for children and wife—
All, all are sleeping, sleeping, sleeping on the hill.

Where are Ella, Kate, Mag, Lizzie, and Edith,
The tender heart, the simple soul, the loud, the proud, the happy one?—
All, all, are sleeping on the hill.

One died in shameful child-birth,
One of a thwarted love,
One at the hands of a brute in a brothel,
One of a broken pride, in a search for a heart's desire,
One after life in faraway London and Paris
Was brought to her little space by Ella and Kate and Mag—
All, all are sleeping, sleeping, sleeping on the hill.

Where are Uncle Isaac and Aunt Emily,
And old Towny Kincaid and Sevigne Houghton,
And Major Walker who had talked
With venerable men of the revolution? —
All, all, are sleeping on the hill.

They brought them dead sons from the war,
And daughters whom life had crushed,
And their children fatherless, crying—
All, all are sleeping, sleeping, sleeping on the hill.

Where is old Fiddler Jones
Who played with life all his ninety years,
Braving the sleet with bared breast,
Drinking, rioting, thinking neither of wife nor kin,
Nor gold, nor love, nor heaven?
Lo! he babbles of the fish-frys of long ago,
Of the horse-races long ago at Clary's Grove,
Of what Abe Lincoln said
One time at Springfield.

A LITANY OF ATLANTA

By

W.E.B. DuBois

W[illiam] E[dward] B[urghardt] Dubois (1868-1963) was born in Great Barrington, Massachusetts, and, in 1896, became the first African-American to receive a Ph.D. from Harvard University. He distinguished himself as a sociologist, author, and civil rights leader. One goal Dubois held was full equality among whites and blacks, and almost all of his writing takes aim at society's racial injustices. He helped found the NAACP in 1909 and believed in social change through agitation and protest, which hindered the overall acceptance of his writings. He moved to Ghana in 1961, after losing faith in the state of race relations in the United States. Dubois died there in 1963

O SILENT GOD, Thou whose voice afar in mist and mystery hath left our ears an hungered in these fearful days-

  Hear us, good Lord!†

 Listen to us, Thy children: our faces dark with doubt are made a mockery in Thy sanctuary. With uplifted hands we front Thy heaven, O God, crying:

  We beseech Thee to hear us, good Lord!

 We are not better than our fellows, Lord, we are but weak and human men. When our devils do deviltry, curse Thou the doer and the deed: curse them as we curse them, do to them all and more than ever they have done to innocence and weakness, to womanhood and home.

  Have mercy upon us, miserable sinners!

And yet whose is the deeper guilt? Who made these devils? Who nursed them in crime and fed them on injustice? Who ravished and debauched their mothers and their grandmothers? Who bought and sold their crime, and waxed fat and rich on public iniquity?

Thou knowest, good God!

Is this Thy justice, O Father, that guile be easier than innocence, and the innocent crucified for the guilt of the untouched guilty?

Justice, O judge of men!

Wherefore do we pray? Is not the God of the fathers dead? Have not seers seen in Heaven's halls Thine hearsed and lifeless form stark amidst the black and rolling smoke of sin; where all along bow bitter forms of endless dead?

Awake, Thou that sleepest!

Thou art not dead, but flown afar, up hills of endless light, thru blazing corridors of suns, where worlds do swing of good and gentle men, of women strong and free-far from the cozenage, black hypocrisy and chaste prostitution of this shameful speck of dust!

Turn again, O Lord, leave us not to perish in our sin!

From lust of body and lust of blood
   Great God, deliver us!

From lust of power and lust of gold,
   Great God, deliver us!

From the leagued lying of despot and of brute,
   Great God, deliver us!

A city lay in travail, God our Lord, and from her loins sprang twin Murder and Black Hate. Red was the midnight; clang, crack and cry of death and fury filled the air and trembled underneath the stars when church spires pointed silently to Thee. And all this was to sate the greed of greedy men who hide behind the veil of vengeance!

Bend us Thine ear, O Lord!

In the pale, still morning we looked upon the deed. We stopped our ears and held our leaping hands, but they-did they not wag their heads and leer and cry with bloody jaws: Cease from Crime! The word was mockery, for thus they train a hundred crimes while we do cure one.

Turn again our captivity, O Lord!

Behold this maimed and broken thing; dear God, it was an humble black man who toiled and sweat to save a bit from the pittance paid him. They told him: Work and Rise. He worked. Did this man sin? Nay, but some one told how some one said another did-one whom he had never seen nor known. Yet for that man's crime this man lieth maimed and murdered, his wife naked to shame, his children, to poverty and evil.

Hear us, O Heavenly Father!

Doth not this justice of hell stink in Thy nostrils, O God? How long shall the mounting flood of innocent blood roar in Thine ears and pound in our hearts for vengeance? Pile the pale frenzy of blood-crazed brutes who do such deeds high on Thine altar, Jehovah Jireh,† and burn it in hell forever and forever!

Forgive us, good Lord; we know not what we say!

Bewildered we are, and passion-tost, mad with the madness of a mobbed and mocked and murdered people; straining at the armposts of Thy Throne, we raise our shackled hands and charge Thee, God, by the bones of our stolen fathers, by the tears of our dead mothers, by the very blood of Thy crucified Christ: What meaneth this? Tell us the Plan; give us the Sign!

Keep not thou silence, O God!

Sit no longer blind, Lord God, deaf to our prayer and dumb to our dumb suffering. Surely Thou too art not white, O Lord, a pale, bloodless, heartless thing?

Ah! Christ of all the Pities!

Forgive the thought! Forgive these wild, blasphemous words. Thou art still the God of our black fathers, and in Thy soul's soul sit some soft darkenings of the evening, some shadowings of the velvet night.

But whisper-speak-call, great God, for Thy silence is white terror to our hearts! The way, O God, show us the way and point us the path.

Whither? North is greed and South is blood; within, the coward, and without, the liar. Whither? To death?
   Amen! Welcome dark sleep!

Whither? To life? But not this life, dear God, not this. Let the cup pass from us, tempt us not beyond our strength, for there is that clamoring and clawing within, to whose voice we would not listen, yet shudder lest we must, and it is red, Ah! God! It is a red and awful shape.
   Selah![†]

In yonder East[†] trembles a star.
   Vengeance is mine; I will repay, saith the Lord!
Thy will, O Lord, be done!
   Kyrie Eleison![†]

Lord, we have done these pleading, wavering words.
   We beseech Thee to hear us, good Lord!

We bow our heads and hearken soft to the sobbing of women and little children.
   We beseech Thee to hear us, good Lord!

Our voices sink in silence and in night.
   Hear us, good Lord!

In night, O God of a godless land!
   Amen!

In silence, O Silent God.
   Selah!

MINIVER CHEEVY

By

Edwin Arlington Robinson

Edwin Arlington Robinson (1869-1935) is a modern writer who won three Pulitzer Prizes for his work. He was born in Gardiner, Maine, the place named Tilbury Town in his poems. He studied at Harvard for two years, but he soon moved to New York City. His cynical view of modern life resounds in his character poems, which are traditional in form, but modern in content. Robinson allowed his friends to support him until his own poetry became popular. He became an alcoholic, like his own "Miniver Cheevey." Robinson published many poems before his death from cancer in a New York City hospital.

Miniver Cheevy, child of scorn,
    Grew lean while he assailed the seasons;
He wept that he was ever born,
    And he had reasons.

Miniver loved the days of old
    When swords were bright and steeds were prancing;
The vision of a warrior bold
    Would send him dancing.

Miniver sighed for what was not,
    And dreamed, and rested from his labors;
He dreamed of Thebes† and Camelot,†
    And Priam's† neighbors.

Miniver mourned the ripe renown
    That made so many a name so fragrant;
He mourned Romance, now on the town,
    And Art, a vagrant.

Miniver loved the Medici,[†]
    Albeit he had never seen one;
He would have sinned incessantly
    Could he have been one.

Miniver cursed the commonplace
    And eyed a khaki suit[†] with loathing:
He missed the medieval grace
    Of iron clothing.[†]

Miniver scorned the gold he sought,
    But sore annoyed was he without it;
Miniver thought, and thought, and thought,
    And thought about it.

Miniver Cheevy, born too late,
    Scratched his head and kept on thinking;
Miniver coughed, and called it fate,
    And kept on drinking.

RICHARD CORY

By

Edwin Arlington Robinson

Whenever Richard Cory went down town,
    We people on the pavement looked at him:
He was a gentleman from sole to crown,
    Clean favored, and imperially slim.

And he was always quietly arrayed,
    And he was always human when he talked;
But still he fluttered pulses when he said,
    "Good-morning," and he glittered when he walked.

And he was rich—yes, richer than a king,
    And admirably schooled in every grace:
In fine, we thought that he was everything
    To make us wish that we were in his place.

So on we worked, and waited for the light,
    And went without the meat, and cursed the bread;
And Richard Cory, one calm summer night,
    Went home and put a bullet through his head.

A MAN ADRIFT ON
A SLIM SPAR

By

Stephen Crane

Stephen Crane (1871-1900), who was born in Newark, New Jersey, is best known as the author of Maggie: A Girl of the Streets, *which Crane self-published in 1893, and* The Red Badge of Courage *(1895). Considered one of America's first realist authors, he also was a journalist and reported on the Greco-Turkish War in 1897. During the Spanish-American War, Crane served as a foreign correspondent in Cuba for Joseph Pulitzer's New York World. His poems are terse, dark parables written in plain speech without decorative elements. This poetic style was unique for his time and helped set the course of American poetry in the twentieth century. Crane died of tuberculosis in Badenweller, Germany, at the age of 29.*

A man adrift on a slim spar
A horizon smaller than the rim of a bottle
Tented waves rearing lashy dark points
The near whine of froth in circles.
        God is cold.

The incessant raise and swing of the sea
And growl after growl of crest
The sinkings, green, seething, endless
The upheaval half-completed.
        God is cold.

The seas are in the hollow of The Hand;[†]
Oceans may be turned to a spray
Raining down through the stars
Because of a gesture of pity toward a babe.
Oceans may become gray ashes,
Die with a long moan and a roar
Amid the tumult of the fishes
And the cries of the ships,
Because The Hand beckons the mice.

A horizon smaller than a doomed assassin's cap,
Inky, surging tumults
A reeling, drunken sky and no sky
A pale hand sliding from a polished spar.
                    God is cold.
The puff of a coat imprisoning air:
A face kissing the water-death
A weary slow sway of a lost hand
And the sea, the moving sea, the sea.
                    God is cold.

A MAN SAID: "THOU TREE!"

By
Stephen Crane

A man said: "Thou tree!"
The tree answered with the same scorn: "Thou man!
Thou art greater than I only in thy possibilities."

I STOOD UPON A HIGH PLACE

By
Stephen Crane

I stood upon a high place,
And saw, below, many devils
Running, leaping,
and carousing in sin.
One looked up, grinning,
And said, "Comrade! Brother!"

IN THE DESERT

By
Stephen Crane

In the desert
I saw a creature, naked, bestial,
Who, squatting upon the ground,
Held his heart in his hands,
And ate of it.
I said, "Is it good, friend?"
"It is bitter—bitter," he answered;
"But I like it
Because it is bitter,
And because it is my heart."

SHOULD THE WIDE WORLD ROLL AWAY

By
Stephen Crane

Should the wide world roll away,
Leaving black terror,
Limitless night,
Nor God, nor man, nor place to stand
Would be to me essential,
If thou and thy white arms were there,
And the fall to doom a long way.

from WAR IS KIND

By

Stephen Crane

Do not weep, maiden, for war is kind.
Because your lover threw wild hands toward the sky
And the affrighted steed[†] ran on alone,
Do not weep.
War is kind.

Hoarse, booming drums of the regiment,
Little souls who thirst for fight,
These men were born to drill and die.
The unexplained glory flies above them,
Great is the battle-god, great, and his kingdom—
A field where a thousand corpses lie.

Do not weep, babe, for war is kind.
Because your father tumbled in the yellow trenches,
Raged at his breast, gulped and died,
Do not weep.
War is kind.

Swift, blazing flag of the regiment,
Eagle with crest of red and gold,
These men were born to drill and die.
Point for them the virtue of slaughter,
Make plain to them the excellence of killing
And a field where a thousand corpses lie.

Mother whose heart hung humble as a button
On the bright splendid shroud of your son,
Do not weep.
War is kind.

LIFT EV'RY VOICE
AND SING

By

James Weldon Johnson

James Weldon Johnson (1871-1938), a leader of the Harlem Renaissance, was born and reared in Jacksonville, Florida. Johnson went to Atlanta University, where he received Bachelor of Arts degree. Later he became a lawyer, passing the Florida bar in 1897—a first for an African-American since the end of Reconstruction. Weldon was politically active, encouraging integration. The NAACP named Johnson's poem, "Lift Ev'ry Voice and Sing" (1899), the Negro National Anthem. The voices in his popular God's Trombones: Seven Negro Sermons in Verse *(1927) are the sounds and rhythms of the southern preachers that Johnson heard as a child. The poems are beautifully melodic and emotionally moving. At the age of 67, Johnson was killed in a car accident in Wiscasset, Maine.*

Lift every voice and sing
Till earth and heaven ring,
Ring with the harmonies of Liberty;
Let our rejoicing rise
High as the listening skies,
Let it resound loud as the rolling sea.
Sing a song full of the faith that the dark past has taught us,
Sing a song full of the hope that the present has brought us.
Facing the rising sun of our new day begun,
Let us march on till victory is won.

Stony the road we trod,
Bitter the chastening rod,
Felt in the days when hope unborn had died;
Yet with a steady beat,
Have not our weary feet
Come to the place for which our fathers sighed?
We have come over a way that with tears have been watered.
We have come, treading our path through the blood of the slaughtered.
Out from the gloomy past,
Till now we stand at last
Where the white gleam of our bright star is cast.

God of our weary years,
God of our silent tears,
Thou who has brought us thus far on the way;
Thou who has by Thy might
Led us into the light,
Keep us forever in the path, we pray.
Lest our feet stray from the places, Our God, where we met Thee;
Lest, our hearts drunk with the wine of the world we forget thee,
Shadowed beneath Thy hand,
May we forever stand,
True to our God,
True to our native land.

THE CREATION

By
James Weldon Johnson

And God stepped out on space,
And he looked around and said:
I'm lonely—
I'll make me a world.

And far as the eye of God could see
Darkness covered everything,
Blacker than a hundred midnights
Down in a cypress swamp.

Then God smiled,
And the light broke,
And the darkness rolled up on one side,
And the light stood shining on the other,
And God said: That's good!

Then God reached out and took the light in his hands,
And God rolled the light around in his hands
Until he made the sun;
And he set that sun a-blazing in the heavens.
And the light that was left from making the sun
God gathered it up in a shining ball
And flung it against the darkness,
Spangling the night with the moon and stars.
Then down between
The darkness and the light
He hurled the world;
And God said: That's good!

Then God himself stepped down—
And the sun was on his right hand,
And the moon was on his left;
The stars were clustered about his head,
And the earth was under his feet.
And God walked, and where he trod
His footsteps hollowed the valleys out
And bulged the mountains up.

Then he stopped and looked and saw
That the earth was hot and barren.
So God stepped over to the edge of the world
And he spat out the seven seas--
He batted his eyes, and the lightnings flashed—
He clapped his hands, and the thunders rolled—
And the waters above the earth came down,
The cooling waters came down.

Then the green grass sprouted,
And the little red flowers blossomed,
The pine tree pointed his finger to the sky,
And the oak spread out his arms,
The lakes cuddled down in the hollows of the ground,
And the rivers ran down to the sea;
And God smiled again,
And the rainbow appeared,
And curled itself around his shoulder.

Then God raised his arm and he waved his hand
Over the sea and over the land,
And he said: Bring forth! Bring forth!
And quicker than God could drop his hand,
Fishes and fowls
And beasts and birds
Swam the rivers and the seas,
Roamed the forests and the woods,
And split the air with their wings.
And God said: That's good!

Then God walked around,
And God looked around
On all that he had made.
He looked at his sun,
And he looked at his moon,
And he looked at his little stars;
He looked on his world
With all its living things,
And God said: I'm lonely still.

Then God sat down—
On the side of a hill where he could think;
By a deep, wide river he sat down;
With his head in his hands,
God thought and thought,
Till he thought: I'll make me a man!

Up from the bed of the river
God scooped the clay;[†]
And by the bank of the river
He kneeled him down;
And there the great God Almighty
Who lit the sun and fixed it in the sky,
Who flung the stars to the most far corner of the night,
Who rounded the earth in the middle of his hand;
This great God,
Like a mammy bending over her baby,
Kneeled down in the dust
Toiling over a lump of clay
Till he shaped it in his own image;

Then into it he blew the breath of life,[†]
And man became a living soul.
Amen. Amen.

MISAPPREHENSION

By

Paul Laurence Dunbar

Paul Laurence Dunbar (1872-1906), born in Dayton, Ohio, was the child of two freed slaves. He became one of the first African-American poets to gain national recognition. By the age of 14, Dunbar had poems published in the Dayton Herald. *Financially unable to attend college, he continued to write poems which finally attracted the attention of critics, other authors, and various literary groups. Dunbar published 12 collections of poems from* Oak and Ivy *(1892) to* The Sport of the Gods *(1902), along with novels, short story collections, and the lyrics to a number of musical reviews. By 1905, he was considered America's premier African-American poet. However, Dunbar suffered from depression stemming from his divorce and tuberculosis. He died in Dayton, Ohio, at the age of 33.*

> Out of my heart, one day, I wrote a song,
>   With my heart's blood imbued,
> Instinct with passion, tremulously strong,
>   With grief subdued;
>   Breathing a fortitude
>   Pain-bought.
> And one who claimed much love for what I wrought,
>   Read and considered it,
>   And spoke:
> "Ay, brother, —'tis well writ,
>   But where's the joke?"

WE WEAR THE MASK

By
Paul Laurence Dunbar

We wear the mask that grins and lies,
It hides our cheeks and shades our eyes,—
This debt we pay to human guile;
With torn and bleeding hearts we smile,
And mouth with myriad subtleties.

Why should the world be over-wise,
In counting all our tears and sighs?
Nay, let them only see us, while
        We wear the mask.

We smile, but, O great Christ, our cries
To Thee from tortured souls arise.
We sing, but oh the clay is vile
Beneath our feet, and long the mile;
But let the world dream otherwise,
        We wear the mask!

HARVEST MOON

By

Josephine Preston Peabody

Josephine Preston Peabody (1874-1922), a talented writer from Dorcester, New York, was successful in writing poems, novels, plays, and short stories. Her first published works appeared in two prestigious magazines, Scribner's *and the* Atlantic Monthly. *Although Peabody had written for years, she developed a depth to her writing when she attended Radcliff College. Peabody traveled widely and then lectured at Wellesley College for two years. After her marriage, she was able to spend more time on her writing. Peabody's feelings about World War I are evident in* Harvest Moon *(1916), her ninth and final volume of poetry. She died at the age of 48 in Cambridge, Massachusetts.*

Over the twilight field,
Over the glimmering field,
And bleeding furrows with their sodden yield
Of sheaves that still did writhe,
After the scythe;
The teeming field and darkly overstrewn
With all the garnered fullness of that noon—
Two looked upon each other.
One was a Woman, men had called their mother:
And one, the Harvest Moon.

And one, the Harvest moon,
Who stood, who gazed
On those unquiet gleanings, where they bled;
Till the lone Woman said:

"But we were crazed...
We should laugh now together, I and you,
We two.
You, for your ever dreaming it was worth
A star's while to look on, and light the Earth;
And I, for ever telling to my mind
Glory it was and gladness, to give birth
To human kind.
I gave the breath,—and thought it not amiss,
I gave the breath to men,
For men to slay again;
Lording it over anguish, all to give
My life, that men might live,
For this.

"You will be laughing now, remembering
We called you once Dead World, and barren thing.
Yes, so we called you then,
You, far more wise
Than to give life to men."

Over the field, that there
Gave back the skies
A shattered upward stare
From sightless eyes,
The furrowed field that lay
Striving awhile, through many a bleeding dune
Of throbbing clay,—but dumb and quiet soon,
She looked; and went her way—
The Harvest Moon.

HARVEST MOON: 1916

By
Josephine Preston Peabody

Moon, slow rising, over the trembling sea-rim,
Moon of the lifted tides and their folded burden,
Look, look down. And gather the blinded oceans,
    Moon of compassion.

Come, white Silence, over the one sea pathway:
Pour with hallowing hands on the surge and outcry,
Silver flame; and over the famished blackness,
    Petals of moonlight.

Once again, the formless void of a world-wreck
Gropes its way through the echoing dark of chaos;
Tide on tide, to the calling, lost horizons,—
    One in the darkness.

You that veil the light of the all-beholding,
Shed white tidings down to the dooms of longing,
Down to the timeless dark; and the sunken treasures,
    One in the darkness.

Touch, and harken,—under that shrouding silver,
Rise and fall, the heart of the sea and its legions,
All and one; one with the breath of the deathless,
    Rising and falling.

Touch and waken so, to a far hereafter,
Ebb and flow, the deep, and the dead in their longing:
Till at last, on the hungering face of the waters,
    There shall be Light.

Light of Light,[†] give us to see, for their sake.
Light of Light, grant them eternal peace;
And let light perpetual shine upon them;
    Light, everlasting.

MADONNA OF THE EVENING FLOWERS

By
Amy Lowell

*Amy Lowell (1874-1925) was from the talented Massachusetts Lowell family;
one of her cousins was the poet James Russell Lowell. Because it was deemed
improper, Lowell did not go to college, but educated herself by reading. Lowell
not only loved reading but also collected volumes, as well. Her family wealth
allowed her to travel widely and write. The Atlantic Monthly published her first
poem in 1910, and she eventually published 13 volumes of poetry. As an Imagist,
Lowell enjoyed writing in free verse. She especially loved John Keats and wrote
a biography of him. Amy Lowell died of a brain hemorrhage when she was only
51 years old.*

> All day long I have been working,
> Now I am tired
> I call: "Where are you?"
> But there is only the oak-tree rustling in the wind.
> The house is very quiet,
> The sun shines in on your books,
> On your scissors and thimble just put down,
> But you are not there.
> Suddenly I am lonely:
> Where are you? I go about searching.

Then I see you,
Standing under a spire of pale blue larkspur,
With a basket of roses on your arm.
You are cool, like silver,
And you smile.
I think the Canterbury bells[†] are playing little tunes.

You tell me that the peonies need spraying,
That the columbines have overrun all bounds,
That the pyrus japonica[†] should be cut back and rounded.
You tell me all these things.
But I look at you, heart of silver,
White heart-flame of polished silver,
Burning beneath the blue steeples of the larkspur,
And I long to kneel instantly at your feet,
While all about us peal the loud, sweet, Te Deums of the
      Canterbury bells.[†]

THE CYCLISTS

By

Amy Lowell

Spread on the roadway,
With open-blown jackets,
Like black, soaring pinions,
They swoop down the hillside,
The Cyclists.
Seeming dark-plumaged
Birds, after carrion,
Careening and circling,
Over the dying
Of England.
She lies with her bosom
Beneath them, no longer
The Dominant Mother,[†]
The Virile—but rotting
Before time.
The smell of her, tainted,
Has bitten their nostrils.
Exultant they hover,
And shadow the sun with
Foreboding.

THE CREMATION OF
SAM MCGEE

By

Robert Service

Robert Service (1874-1958) was a Scottish-born writer who lived in England until his twenties, when he moved to Canada and became a banker. Living in the Yukon Territory gave Service a great love and enthusiasm for its wild and expansive beauty. His poetry reflects this inspiration. For example, "The Shooting of Dan McGrew" and "The Cremation of Sam McGee," are collected in The Spell of the Yukon and Other Verse *(1907). He produced 45 collections of poetry. His writing gave him wealth, which he used to travel and then live on the French Riviera, where he died at the age of 84.*

There are strange things done in the midnight sun
By the men who moil for gold;
The Arctic trails have their secret tales
That would make your blood run cold;
The Northern Lights[†] have seen queer sights,
But the queerest they ever did see
Was that night on the marge of Lake Lebarge[†]
I cremated Sam McGee.

Now Sam McGee was from Tennessee, where the cotton blooms and blows.
Why he left his home in the South to roam 'round the Pole, God only
  knows.
He was always cold, but the land of gold seemed to hold him like a spell;
Though he'd often say in his homely way that he'd "sooner live in hell".

On a Christmas Day we were mushing our way over the Dawson trail.†
Talk of your cold! through the parka's fold it stabbed like a driven nail.
If our eyes we'd close, then the lashes froze till sometimes we couldn't see;
It wasn't much fun, but the only one to whimper was Sam McGee.

And that very night, as we lay packed tight in our robes beneath the snow,
And the dogs were fed, and the stars o'erhead were dancing heel and toe,
He turned to me, and "Cap," says he, "I'll cash in this trip, I guess;
And if I do, I'm asking that you won't refuse my last request."

Well, he seemed so low that I couldn't say no; then he says with a sort of
  moan:
"It's the cursed cold, and it's got right hold till I'm chilled clean through to
  the bone.
Yet 'tain't being dead—it's my awful dread of the icy grave that pains;
So I want you to swear that, foul or fair, you'll cremate my last remains."

A pal's last need is a thing to heed, so I swore I would not fail;
And we started on at the streak of dawn; but God! he looked ghastly pale.
He crouched on the sleigh, and he raved all day of his home in Tennessee;
And before nightfall a corpse was all that was left of Sam McGee.

There wasn't a breath in that land of death, and I hurried, horror-driven,
With a corpse half hid that I couldn't get rid, because of a promise given;
It was lashed to the sleigh, and it seemed to say:
"You may tax your brawn and brains,
But you promised true, and it's up to you to cremate those last remains."

Now a promise made is a debt unpaid, and the trail has its own stern code.
In the days to come, though my lips were dumb, in my heart how I cursed
  that load.
In the long, long night, by the lone firelight, while the huskies, round in a
  ring,
Howled out their woes to the homeless snows—O God! how I loathed the
  thing.

And every day that quiet clay seemed to heavy and heavier grow;
And on I went, though the dogs were spent and the grub was getting low;
The trail was bad, and I felt half mad, but I swore I would not give in;
And I'd often sing to the hateful thing, and it hearkened with a grin.

Till I came to the marge of Lake Lebarge, and a derelict there lay;
It was jammed in the ice, but I saw in a trice it was called the "Alice May".
And I looked at it, and I thought a bit, and I looked at my frozen chum;
Then "Here," said I, with a sudden cry, "is my cre-ma-tor-eum."

Some planks I tore from the cabin floor, and I lit the boiler fire;
Some coal I found that was lying around, and I heaped the fuel higher;
The flames just soared, and the furnace roared—such a blaze you seldom
     see;
And I burrowed a hole in the glowing coal, and I stuffed in Sam McGee.

Then I made a hike, for I didn't like to hear him sizzle so;
And the heavens scowled, and the huskies howled, and the wind began to
     blow.
It was icy cold, but the hot sweat rolled down my cheeks, and I don't know
     why;
And the greasy smoke in an inky cloak went streaking down the sky.

I do not know how long in the snow I wrestled with grisly fear;
But the stars came out and they danced about ere again I ventured near;
I was sick with dread, but I bravely said: "I'll just take a peep inside.
I guess he's cooked, and it's time I looked";…then the door I opened wide.

And there sat Sam, looking cool and calm, in the heart of the furnace roar;
And he wore a smile you could see a mile, and he said: "Please close that
     door.
It's fine in here, but I greatly fear you'll let in the cold and storm—
Since I left Plumtree, down in Tennessee, it's the first time I've been warm."

There are strange things done in the midnight sun
By the men who moil for gold;
The Arctic trails have their secret tales
That would make your blood run cold;
The Northern Lights have seen queer sights,
But the queerest they ever did see
Was that night on the marge of Lake Lebarge
I cremated Sam McGee.

THE DEATH OF THE HIRED MAN

By

Robert Frost

Robert Frost (1874-1963) was one of the most popular poets of the 20th century. Many remember the day he recited "The Gift Outright" at John F. Kennedy's inauguration (1961). Although Frost was born in San Francisco, he spent most of his life in New England. He studied at Dartmouth and Harvard, but did not complete his class work. His themes come from his life experiences as a New England farmer and teacher. Frost's works span most of the first half of the century, beginning with the publication of A Boy's Will *(1913) while he was in England. On the surface, his poems appear simple, containing country scenes and language, but his brilliance is in the fact that his poetry is quite complex. Frost received an abundance of awards, including many honorary degrees and four Pulitzer Prizes, but never captured the Nobel Prize for Literature. Frost died in Boston at the age of 88.*

Mary sat musing on the lamp-flame at the table
Waiting for Warren. When she heard his step,
She ran on tip-toe down the darkened passage
To meet him in the doorway with the news
And put him on his guard. "Silas is back."
She pushed him outward with her through the door
And shut it after her. "Be kind," she said.
She took the market things from Warren's arms

And set them on the porch, then drew him down
To sit beside her on the wooden steps.

"When was I ever anything but kind to him?
But I'll not have the fellow back," he said.
"I told him so last haying, didn't I?
'If he left then,' I said, 'that ended it.'
What good is he? Who else will harbour him
At his age for the little he can do?
What help he is there's no depending on.
Off he goes always when I need him most.
'He thinks he ought to earn a little pay,
Enough at least to buy tobacco with,
So he won't have to beg and be beholden.'
'All right,' I say, 'I can't afford to pay
Any fixed wages, though I wish I could.'
'Someone else can.' 'Then someone else will have to.'
I shouldn't mind his bettering himself
If that was what it was. You can be certain,
When he begins like that, there's someone at him
Trying to coax him off with pocket-money,—
In haying time, when any help is scarce.
In winter he comes back to us. I'm done."

"Sh! not so loud: he'll hear you," Mary said.

"I want him to: he'll have to soon or late."

"He's worn out. He's asleep beside the stove.
When I came up from Rowe's I found him here,
Huddled against the barn-door fast asleep,
A miserable sight, and frightening, too—
You needn't smile—I didn't recognise him—
I wasn't looking for him—and he's changed.
Wait till you see."

                    "Where did you say he'd been?"

"He didn't say. I dragged him to the house,
And gave him tea and tried to make him smoke.
I tried to make him talk about his travels.
Nothing would do: he just kept nodding off."

"What did he say? Did he say anything?"

"But little."

                    "Anything? Mary, confess
He said he'd come to ditch the meadow for me."

"Warren!"

                "But did he? I just want to know."

"Of course he did. What would you have him say?
Surely you wouldn't grudge the poor old man
Some humble way to save his self-respect.
He added, if you really care to know,
He meant to clear the upper pasture, too.
That sounds like something you have heard before?
Warren, I wish you could have heard the way
He jumbled everything. I stopped to look
Two or three times—he made me feel so queer—
To see if he was talking in his sleep.
He ran on Harold Wilson—you remember—
The boy you had in haying four years since.
He's finished school, and teaching in his college.
Silas declares you'll have to get him back.
He says they two will make a team for work:
Between them they will lay this farm as smooth!
The way he mixed that in with other things.
He thinks young Wilson a likely lad, though daft
On education—you know how they fought
All through July under the blazing sun,
Silas up on the cart to build the load,
Harold along beside to pitch it on."

"Yes, I took care to keep well out of earshot."

"Well, those days trouble Silas like a dream.
You wouldn't think they would. How some things linger!
Harold's young college boy's assurance piqued him.
After so many years he still keeps finding
Good arguments he sees he might have used.
I sympathise. I know just how it feels
To think of the right thing to say too late.

Harold's associated in his mind with Latin.
He asked me what I thought of Harold's saying
He studied Latin like the violin
Because he liked it—that an argument!
He said he couldn't make the boy believe
He could find water with a hazel prong[†]—
Which showed how much good school had ever done him.
He wanted to go over that. But most of all
He thinks if he could have another chance
To teach him how to build a load of hay——"

"I know, that's Silas' one accomplishment.
He bundles every forkful in its place,
And tags and numbers it for future reference,
So he can find and easily dislodge it
In the unloading. Silas does that well.
He takes it out in bunches like big birds' nests.
You never see him standing on the hay
He's trying to lift, straining to lift himself."
"He thinks if he could teach him that, he'd be
Some good perhaps to someone in the world.
He hates to see a boy the fool of books.
Poor Silas, so concerned for other folk,
And nothing to look backward to with pride,
And nothing to look forward to with hope,
So now and never any different."

Part of a moon was falling down the west,
Dragging the whole sky with it to the hills.
Its light poured softly in her lap. She saw
And spread her apron to it. She put out her hand
Among the harp-like morning-glory strings,
Taut with the dew from garden bed to eaves,
As if she played unheard the tenderness
That wrought on him beside her in the night.
"Warren," she said, "he has come home to die:
You needn't be afraid he'll leave you this time."

"Home," he mocked gently.

                              "Yes, what else but home?
It all depends on what you mean by home.

Of course he's nothing to us, any more
Than was the hound that came a stranger to us
Out of the woods, worn out upon the trail."

"Home is the place where, when you have to go there,
They have to take you in."

                    "I should have called it
Something you somehow haven't to deserve."

Warren leaned out and took a step or two,
Picked up a little stick, and brought it back
And broke it in his hand and tossed it by.
"Silas has better claim on us you think
Than on his brother? Thirteen little miles
As the road winds would bring him to his door.
Silas has walked that far no doubt to-day.
Why didn't he go there? His brother's rich,
A somebody—director in the bank."

"He never told us that."

                    "We know it though."

"I think his brother ought to help, of course.
I'll see to that if there is need. He ought of right
To take him in, and might be willing to—
He may be better than appearances.
But have some pity on Silas. Do you think
If he'd had any pride in claiming kin
Or anything he looked for from his brother,
He'd keep so still about him all this time?"

"I wonder what's between them."

                    "I can tell you.
Silas is what he is—we wouldn't mind him—
But just the kind that kinsfolk can't abide.
He never did a thing so very bad.
He don't know why he isn't quite as good
As anyone. He won't be made ashamed
To please his brother, worthless though he is."

"I can't think Si ever hurt anyone."

"No, but he hurt my heart the way he lay
And rolled his old head on that sharp-edged chair-back.
He wouldn't let me put him on the lounge.
You must go in and see what you can do.
I made the bed up for him there to-night.
You'll be surprised at him—how much he's broken.
His working days are done; I'm sure of it."

"I'd not be in a hurry to say that."

"I haven't been. Go, look, see for yourself.
But, Warren, please remember how it is:
He's come to help you ditch the meadow.
He has a plan. You mustn't laugh at him.
He may not speak of it, and then he may.
I'll sit and see if that small sailing cloud
Will hit or miss the moon."

　　　　　　　　　It hit the moon.

Then there were three there, making a dim row,
The moon, the little silver cloud, and she.

Warren returned—too soon, it seemed to her,
Slipped to her side, caught up her hand and waited.

"Warren," she questioned.

　　　　　　　　"Dead," was all he answered.

FIRE AND ICE

By
Robert Frost

Some say the world will end in fire,
Some say in ice.
From what I've tasted of desire
I hold with those who favor fire.
But if it had to perish twice,
I think I know enough of hate
To know that for destruction ice
Is also great
And would suffice.

THE ROAD NOT TAKEN

By
Robert Frost

Two roads diverged in a yellow wood,
And sorry I could not travel both
And be one traveler, long I stood
And looked down one as far as I could
To where it bent in the undergrowth;

Then took the other, as just as fair,
And having perhaps the better claim,
Because it was grassy and wanted wear;
Though as for that the passing there
Had worn them really about the same,

And both that morning equally lay
In leaves no step had trodden black.
Oh, I kept the first for another day!
Yet knowing how way leads on to way,
I doubted if I should ever come back.

I shall be telling this with a sigh
Somewhere ages and ages hence:
Two roads diverged in a wood, and I—
I took the one less traveled by,
And that has made all the difference.

TWO TRAMPS IN MUD TIME

By
Robert Frost

Out of the mud two strangers came
And caught me splitting wood in the yard.
And one of them put me off my aim
By hailing cheerily "Hit them hard!"
I knew pretty well why he had dropped behind
And let the other go on a way.
I knew pretty well what he had in mind:
He wanted to take my job for pay.

Good blocks of oak it was I split,
As large around as the chopping block;
And every piece I squarely hit
Fell splinterless as a cloven rock.
The blows that a life of self-control
Spares to strike for the common good
That day, giving a loose my soul,
I spent on the unimportant wood.

The sun was warm but the wind was chill.
You know how it is with an April day:
When the sun is out and the wind is still,
You're one month on in the middle of May.
But if you so much as dare to speak,
A cloud comes over the sunlit arch,
A wind comes off a frozen peak,
And you're two months back in the middle of March.

A bluebird comes tenderly up to alight
And turns to the wind to unruffle a plume,
His song so pitched as not to excite
A single flower as yet to bloom.
It is snowing a flake: and he half knew
Winter was only playing possum.[†]
Except in color he isn't blue,
But he wouldn't advise a thing to blossom.

The water for which we may have to look

In summertime with a witching-wand,[†]
In every wheelrut's now a brook,
In every print of a hoof a pond.
Be glad of water, but don't forget
The lurking frost in the earth beneath
That will steal forth after the sun is set
And show on the water its crystal teeth.

The time when most I loved my task
The two must make me love it more
By coming with what they came to ask.
You'd think I never had felt before
The weight of an ax-head poised aloft,
The grip of earth on outspread feet,
The life of muscles rocking soft
And smooth and moist in vernal heat.

Out of the wood two hulking tramps
(From sleeping God knows where last night
But not long since in the lumber camps).
They thought all chopping was theirs of right.
Men of the woods and lumberjacks,
The judged me by their appropriate tool.
Except as a fellow handled an ax
They had no way of knowing a fool.

Nothing on either side was said.
They knew they had but to stay their stay
And all their logic would fill my head:
As that I had no right to play
With what was another man's work for gain.
My right might be love but theirs was need.
And where the two exist in twain
Theirs was the better right—agreed.

But yield who will to their separation,
My object in living is to unite
My avocation and my vocation
As my two eyes make one in sight.
Only where love and need are one,
And the work is play for mortal stakes,
Is the deed ever really done
For Heaven and the future's sakes.

I Sit and Sew

By
Alice Moore Dunbar-Nelson

Alice Moore Dunbar-Nelson (1875-1935) was born in New Orleans. She was descended from African-American, Native American, and European heritage. Because of her diverse background, she gained access to the entire gamut of racial and ethnic classes that existed in New Orleans and other American cities at the time. Dunbar-Nelson was, at various times in her life, a short fiction writer, poet, diarist, journalist, editor, teacher, political activist, and public speaker. Her literary works deal with romantic themes, and she frequently points out differences in social class without introducing the element of race or gender, although these themes are present in a collection of her essays, published posthumously. She married three times; the first was to the poet Paul Laurence Dunbar, but it was a difficult, tumultuous, and sometimes abusive marriage that ended in divorce. Alice Moore Dunbar-Nelson suffered a heart attack and died in 1935.

> I sit and sew—a useless task it seems,
> My hands grown tired, my head weighed down with dreams—
> The panoply of war, the martial tread of men,
> Grim-faced, stern-eyed, gazing beyond the ken
> Of lesser souls, whose eyes have not seen Death
> Nor learned to hold their lives but as a breath—
> But—I must sit and sew.

I sit and sew—my heart aches with desire—
That pageant terrible, that fiercely pouring fire
On wasted fields, and writhing grotesque things[†]
Once men. My soul in pity flings
Appealing cries, yearning only to go
There in that holocaust of hell, those fields of woe—
But—I must sit and sew.

The little useless seam, the idle patch;
Why dream I here beneath my homely thatch,
When there they lie in sodden mud and rain,
Pitifully calling me, the quick ones and the slain?
You need me, Christ! It is no roseate dream
That beckons me—this pretty futile seam,
It stifles me—God, must I sit and sew?

GRANDMITHER,
THINK NOT I FORGET

By
Willa Cather

Willa Cather (1876-1947) left her birthplace of Back Creek Valley, Virginia, at ten years of age to begin homesteading with her family in Nebraska. During college at the University of Nebraska, she wrote drama critiques for the school paper and acted in a number of plays. Cather had a successful career writing essays, poems, short stories, novels, as well as writing for and editing newspapers and magazines. Critics consider one of her most famous works, My Ántonia, *a "masterpiece of narrative perspective." She lectured throughout the country extensively and was the first woman to be inducted into the Nebraska Hall of Fame. Cather died in New York City of a cerebral hemorrhage on April 24, 1947.*

Grandmither, think not I forget, when I come back to town,
An' wander the old ways again, an' tread them up and down.
I never smell the clover bloom, nor see the swallows pass,
Without I mind how good ye were unto a little lass.
I never hear the winter rain a-pelting all night through,
Without I think and mind me of how cold it falls on you.
And if I come not often to your bed beneath the thyme,
Mayhap[†] 'tis that I'd change wi' ye, and gie[†] my bed for thine,
      Would like to sleep in thine.

I never hear the summer winds among the roses blow,
Without I wonder why it was ye loved the lassie so.
Ye gave me cakes and lollipops and pretty toys a score,—
I never thought I should come back and ask ye now for more.
Grandmither, gie me your still, white hands, that lie upon your breast,
For mine do beat the dark all night, and never find me rest;
They grope among the shadows an' they beat the cold black air,
They go seekin' in the darkness, an' they never find him there,
      They never find him there.

Grandmither, gie me your sightless eyes, that I may never see
His own a-burnin' full o' love that must not shine for me.
Grandmither, gie me your peaceful lips, white as the kirkyard snow,
For mine be red wi' burnin' thirst an' he must never know.
Grandmither, gie me your clay-stopped ears, that I may never hear
My lad a-singin' in the night when I am sick wi' fear;
A-singin' when the moonlight over a' the land is white—
Ah, God! I'll up an' go to him a-singin' in the night,
      A-callin' in the night.

Grandmither, gie me your clay-cold heart that has forgot to ache
For mine be fire within my breast and yet it cannot break.
It beats an' throbs forever for things that must not be,—
An' can ye not let me creep in an' rest awhile by ye?
A little lass afeard o' dark slept by ye years agone—
Ah, she has found what night can hold 'twixt sundown an' the dawn!†
So when I plant the rose an' rue above your grave for ye,
Ye'll know it's under rue an' rose that I would like to be,
      That I would like to be.

CHICAGO

By
Carl Sandburg

Carl Sandburg (1878-1967), called "The Voice of the Industrial Revolution," was one of the most versatile modern writers. He was born in Galesburg, Illinois, and later studied at Lombard College. Sandburg's travels produced The American Songbag, *a preservation of American folk song. He was acclaimed for his biographies of Abraham Lincoln (his boyhood hero) for which he won the Pulitzer Prize in 1939.* Rootabaga Stories *were written for children, but he is most famous for his poems about industrial Chicago and the workingman. Sandburg won another Pulitzer for* Complete Poems *(1950). He died of a heart attack in his home in Flat Rock, North Carolina.*

Hog Butcher for the World,[†]
Tool Maker, Stacker of Wheat,
Player with Railroads and the Nation's Freight Handler;
Stormy, husky, brawling,
City of the Big Shoulders:

They tell me you are wicked and I believe them, for I have seen your
        painted women[†] under the gas lamps luring the farm boys.
And they tell me you are crooked and I answer: Yes, it is true I have seen
        the gunman kill and go free to kill again.
And they tell me you are brutal and my reply is: On the faces of women
        and children I have seen the marks of wanton hunger.

And having answered so I turn once more to those who sneer at this my
     city, and I give them back the sneer and say to them:
Come and show me another city with lifted head singing so proud to be
     alive and coarse and strong and cunning.
Flinging magnetic curses amid the toil of piling job on job, here is a tall
     bold slugger set vivid against the little soft cities;
Fierce as a dog with tongue lapping for action, cunning as a savage pitted
     against the wilderness,
          Bareheaded,
          Shoveling,
          Wrecking,
          Planning,
          Building, breaking, rebuilding,
Under the smoke, dust all over his mouth, laughing with white teeth,
Under the terrible burden of destiny laughing as a young man laughs,
Laughing even as an ignorant fighter laughs who has never lost a battle,
Bragging and laughing that under his wrist is the pulse, and under his ribs
     the heart of the people,
          Laughing!
Laughing the stormy, husky, brawling laughter of Youth, half-naked,
     sweating, proud to be Hog Butcher, Tool Maker, Stacker of Wheat,
     Player with Railroads and Freight Handler to the Nation.

CHICAGO POET

By
Carl Sandburg

I SALUTED a nobody.
I saw him in a looking-glass.
He smiled—so did I.
He crumpled the skin on his forehead,
    frowning—so did I.
Everything I did he did.
I said, "Hello, I know you."
And I was a liar to say so.

Ah, this looking-glass man!
Liar, fool, dreamer, play-actor,
Soldier, dusty drinker of dust—
Ah! he will go with me
Down the dark stairway
When nobody else is looking,
When everybody else is gone.

He locks his elbow in mine,
I lose all—but not him.

FOG

By
Carl Sandburg

The fog comes
on little cat feet.

It sits looking
over harbor and city
on silent haunches
and then moves on.

GRASS

By
Carl Sandburg

Pile the bodies high at Austerlitz[†] and Waterloo.[†]
Shovel them under and let me work –
    I am the grass; I cover all.

And pile them high at Gettysburg[†]
And pile them high at Ypres[†] and Verdun.[†]
Shovel them under and let me work.
Two years, ten years, and passengers ask the conductor:
    What place is this?
    Where are we now?

    I am the grass.
    Let me work.

SHENANDOAH

By
Carl Sandburg

In the Shenandoah Valley,[†] one rider gray and one rider blue,[†] and the sun
on the riders wondering.

Piled in the Shenandoah, riders blue and riders gray, piled with shovels,
one and another, dust in the Shenandoah taking them quicker
than mothers take children done with play.

The blue nobody remembers, the gray nobody remembers, it's all old and
old nowadays in the Shenandoah.

And all is young, a butter of dandelions slung on the turf, climbing blue
flowers of the wishing woodlands wondering: a midnight purple
violet claims the sun among old heads, among old dreams of
repeating heads of a rider blue and a rider gray in the Shenandoah
.

SMOKE

By
Carl Sandburg

I sit in a chair and read the newspapers.

Millions of men go to war, acres of them are buried, guns and ships
broken, cities burned, villages sent up in smoke, and children
where cows are killed off amid hoarse barbecues vanish like
finger-rings of smoke in a north wind.

I sit in a chair and read the newspapers.

GENERAL WILLIAM BOOTH[†]
ENTERS INTO HEAVEN

By

Vachel Lindsay

Vachel Lindsay (1879-1931) wrote in the popular style of other early 20th Century writers, such as Carl Sandburg. Lindsay lived in Springfield, Illinois, but for many years he traveled, selling and reciting his poems. His oratorical presentations made him more popular than his poetry did. His two most praised poems are "The Congo" and "General Booth Enters Heaven." Lindsay was suffered from epilepsy and mental health issues. On December 5, 1931, he died after drinking Lysol.

I

(*Bass drum beaten loudly.*)
Booth led boldly with his big bass drum—
(Are you washed in the blood of the Lamb?)[†]
The Saints smiled gravely and they said: "He's come."
(Are you washed in the blood of the Lamb?)
Walking lepers followed, rank on rank,
Lurching bravoes from the ditches dank,
Drabs from the alleyways and drug fiends pale—
Minds still passion-ridden, soul-powers frail:—
Vermin-eaten saints with mouldy breath,
Unwashed legions with the ways of Death—
(Are you washed in the blood of the Lamb?)

(*Banjos.*)
Every slum had sent its half-a-score[†]
The round world over. (Booth had groaned for more.)
Every banner that the wide world flies
Bloomed with glory and transcendent dyes.
Big-voiced lasses made their banjos bang,[†]
Tranced, fanatical they shrieked and sang:—
"Are you washed in the blood of the Lamb?"
Hallelujah! It was queer to see
Bull-necked convicts with that land make free.
Loons with trumpets blowed a blare, blare, blare
On, on upward thro' the golden air!
(Are you washed in the blood of the Lamb?)

II

(*Bass drum slower and softer.*)
Booth died blind and still by Faith he trod,
Eyes still dazzled by the ways of God.
Booth led boldly, and he looked the chief
Eagle countenance in sharp relief,
Beard a-flying, air of high command
Unabated in that holy land.

(*Sweet flute music.*)
Jesus came from out the court-house door,
Stretched his hands above the passing poor.
Booth saw not, but led his queer ones there
Round and round the mighty court-house square.
Then in an instant all that blear review
Marched on spotless, clad in raiment new.
The lame were straightened, withered limbs uncurled
And blind eyes opened on a new, sweet world.

(*Bass drum louder.*)
Drabs and vixens in a flash made whole!
Gone was the weasel-head, the snout, the jowl!
Sages and sibyls now, and athletes clean,
Rulers of empires, and of forests green!

(*Grand chorus of all instruments. Tambourines to the foreground.*)
The hosts were sandaled, and their wings were fire!
(Are you washed in the blood of the Lamb?)
But their noise played havoc with the angel-choir.
(Are you washed in the blood of the Lamb?)
Oh, shout Salvation! It was good to see
Kings and Princes by the Lamb set free.
The banjos rattled and the tambourines
Jing-jing-jingled in the hands of Queens.

(*Reverently sung, no instruments.*)
And when Booth halted by the curb for prayer
He saw his Master thro' the flag-filled air.
Christ came gently with a robe and crown
For Booth the soldier, while the throng knelt down.
He saw King Jesus. They were face to face,
And he knelt a-weeping in that holy place.
Are you washed in the blood of the Lamb?

THE EMPEROR OF
ICE-CREAM

By

Wallace Stevens

Wallace Stevens (1879-1955), considered one of the outstanding poets of modern time, was a full-time businessman and part-time poet. His first poems were printed in Poetry *magazine (1914). Stevens won the prestigious Pulitzer Prize (1955) for his work. Emphasizing the imagination, Stevens wrote much of his poetry after the age of 35. He died in Hartford, Connecticut, of stomach cancer.*

Call the roller of big cigars,
The muscular one, and bid him whip
In kitchen cups concupiscent curds.
Let the wenches dawdle in such dress
As they are used to wear, and let the boys
Bring flowers in last month's newspapers.
Let be be finale of seem.
The only emperor is the emperor of ice-cream.
Take from the dresser of deal,[†]
Lacking the three glass knobs, that sheet
On which she embroidered fantails once
And spread it so as to cover her face.
If her horny feet protrude, they come
To show how cold she is, and dumb.
Let the lamp affix its beam.
The only emperor is the emperor of ice-cream.

LET ME LIVE OUT MY YEARS

By

John G. Neihardt

John G. Neihardt (1881-1973) is one of the only American poets associated with the Great Plains. He was born in Sharpsburg, Illinois, and lived for a brief time in a sod house on the prairie in Kansas. After receiving his education at the Nebraska Normal College, he taught school and continued his writing. Traveling the West and interviewing longtime inhabitants became the basis for most of his writing. Neihardt's volume of work preserves the last days of the frontier for posterity. He died at the age of 91 in Columbus, Missouri.

LET me live out my years in heat of blood!
Let me die drunken with the dreamer's wine!
Let me not see this soul-house built of mud
Go toppling to the dusk—a vacant shrine.

Let me go quickly, like a candle light
Snuffed out just at the heyday of its glow.
Give me high noon—and let it then be night!
Thus would I go.

And grant that when I face the grisly Thing,[†]
My song may trumpet down the gray Perhaps.
Let me be as a tune-swept fiddlestring
That feels the Master Melody—and snaps!

THE RED WHEELBARROW

By
William Carlos Williams

William Carlos Williams (1883-1963) began his career in high school and became one of the main Imagists of the 20th century and a prolific writer of poetry, novels, short stories, essays, and translations. Williams was born in Rutherford, New York, and educated at the University of Pennsylvania, where he earned an M.D. He went on to establish an outstanding career in medicine. His first work, Poems, was published in 1909. Moving away from Imagist poetry, Williams created his own American style and idea of poetry. He had a heart attack in 1948, followed by a series of strokes. His mental and physical health continued to deteriorate, and Williams died in 1963 at age 79.

> so much depends
> upon
>
> a red wheel
> barrow
>
> glazed with rain
> water
>
> beside the white
> chickens

THIS IS JUST TO SAY

By
William Carlos Williams

I have eaten
the plums
that were in
the icebox

and which
you were probably
saving
for breakfast

Forgive me
they were delicious
so sweet
and so cold

I SHALL NOT CARE

By

Sara Teasdale

Sara Teasdale (1884-1933) was a prize-winning poet, known for her lyrical poetry, which often dealt with the Romantic themes of the 1800s. Teasdale was born in St. Louis, Missouri. Although in poor health during childhood, she received a substantial education, graduating from Hosner Hall in 1903. Teasdale's poems reflect internal life, as her marriage and social life were unhappy. She published four volumes of poems; the last, Strange Victory, *appeared posthumously. At 49 years old, Sara Teasdale died of an overdose of sleeping pills.*

When I am dead and over me bright April
    Shakes out her rain-drenched hair,
Though you shall lean above me broken-hearted,
    I shall not care.

I shall have peace as leafy trees are peaceful,
    When rain bends down the bough,
And I shall be more silent and cold-hearted
    Than you are now.

THE KISS

By
Sara Teasdale

Before you kissed me only winds of heaven
Had kissed me, and the tenderness of rain—
Now you have come, how can I care for kisses
Like theirs again? I sought the sea, she sent her winds to meet me,
They surged about me singing of the south—
I turned my head away to keep still holy
Your kiss upon my mouth. And swift sweet rains of shining April weather
Found not my lips where living kisses are;
I bowed my head lest they put out my glory
As rain puts out a star. I am my love's and he is mine forever,
Sealed with a seal and safe forevermore—
Think you that I could let a beggar enter
Where a king stood before?

THE PROUD POET
(For Shaemas O'Sheel)[†]

By

Joyce Kilmer

Joyce Kilmer (1886-1918) is known mainly for his poem "Trees." He was also the most outstanding Catholic writer and lecturer of his time. Kilmer was from Brunswick, New Jersey. Coming from a privileged home gave him the opportunity to attend Rutgers Preparatory School, then Rutgers College. After his daughter Rose contracted polio, Kilmer searched for faith, which he found in the Catholic Church. Enlisting for World War I, he chose the most dangerous assignments by joining the Regimental Intelligence Section. One day on a reconnaissance mission, Kilmer was shot and died instantly. He wrote many poems, which were published in several volumes; at least two were published posthumously.

One winter night a Devil came and sat upon my bed,
His eyes were full of laughter for his heart was full of crime.
"Why don't you take up fancy work, or embroidery?" he said,
"For a needle is as manly a tool as a pen that makes a rhyme!"
"You little ugly Devil," said I, "go back to Hell
For the idea you express I will not listen to:
I have trouble enough with poetry and poverty as well,
Without having to pay attention to orators like you.
"When you say of the making of ballads and songs that it is woman's work
You forget all the fighting poets that have been in every land.
There was Byron[†] who left all his lady-loves to fight against the Turk,[†]

And David, the Singing King of the Jews,[†]
 who was born with a sword in his hand.
It was yesterday that Rupert Brooke[†] went out to the Wars and died,
And Sir Philip Sidney's[†] lyric voice was as sweet as his arm was strong;
And Sir Walter Raleigh[†] met the axe as a lover meets his bride,
Because he carried in his soul the courage of his song.
"And there is no consolation so quickening to the heart
As the warmth and whiteness that come from the lines of noble poetry.
It is strong joy to read it when the wounds of the spirit smart,
It puts the flame in a lonely breast where only ashes be.
It is strong joy to read it, and to make it is a thing
That exalts a man with a sacreder pride than any pride on earth.
For it makes him kneel to a broken slave and set his foot on a king,
And it shakes the walls of his little soul with the echo of God's mirth.
"There was the poet Homer[†] had the sorrow to be blind,
Yet a hundred people with good eyes would listen to him all night;
For they took great enjoyment in the heaven of his mind,
And were glad when the old blind poet let them share his powers of sight.
And there was Heine[†] lying on his mattress all day long,
He had no wealth, he had no friends, he had no joy at all,
Except to pour his sorrow into little cups of song,
And the world finds in them the magic wine that his broken heart let fall.
"And these are only a couple of names from a list of a thousand score
Who have put their glory on the world in poverty and pain.
And the title of poet's a noble thing, worth living and dying for,
Though all the devils on earth and in Hell spit at me their disdain.
It is stern work, it is perilous work, to thrust your hand in the sun
And pull out a spark of immortal flame to warm the hearts of men:
But Prometheus, torn[†] by the claws and beaks whose task is never done,
Would be tortured another eternity to go stealing fire again."

TREES

By
Joyce Kilmer

I think that I shall never see
A poem lovely as a tree.

A tree whose hungry mouth is prest
Against the sweet earth's flowing breast;

A tree that looks at God all day,
And lifts her leafy arms to pray;

A tree that may in summer wear
A nest of robins in her hair;

Upon whose bosom snow has lain;
Who intimately lives with rain.

Poems are made by fools like me,
But only God can make a tree.

OREAD

By
H.D.

H[ilda] D[oolittle] (1886-1961) was part of the Imagist Movement of the 20th century, but later in life created her own unique style. Born in Bethlehem, Pennsylvania, and educated at Bryn Mawr College and the University of Pennsylvania, H.D. traveled to Europe in 1911, never returning to the United States. The poet Ezra Pound was not only her companion, but also a huge influence on her poetry. H.D.'s first poems were published in the magazine, Poetry, in 1913. Much of her poetry reflects her adoration for Greek art, literature, and history. Throughout her life, H.D. suffered poor mental health, which culminated in a nervous breakdown in 1944; however, she continued to write a great deal of poetry. She is considered one of the most outstanding women of the Imagist Movement. She died of a stroke in Switzerland at the age of 77.

> Whirl up, sea—
> whirl your pointed pines,
> splash your great pines
> on our rocks,
> hurl your green over us,
> cover us with your pools of fir.

I HAVE A RENDEZVOUS WITH DEATH

By
Alan Seeger

Alan Seeger (1888-1916) was born in New York and educated at Harvard, but he chose to live a bohemian lifestyle in Greenwich Village and the Parisian Latin Quarter. Seeger's one volume, called Poems, *was published posthumously. His most famous poem is "Rendezvous," which foreshadows a person's death. Ironically, Seeger joined the French Foreign Legion, and in 1916, was killed in battle before the poem was ever read.*

> I have a rendezvous with Death
> At some disputed barricade,
> When Spring comes back with rustling shade
> And apple-blossoms fill the air—
> I have a rendezvous with Death
> When Spring brings back blue days and fair.
>
> It may be he shall take my hand,
> And lead me into his dark land,
> And close my eyes and quench my breath—
> It may be I shall pass him still.
> I have a rendezvous with Death
> On some scarred slope of battered hill,
> When Spring comes round again this year
> And the first meadow flowers appear.

God knows 'twere better to be deep
Pillowed in silk and scented down,
Where love throbs out in blissful sleep,
Pulse nigh to pulse, and breath to breath,
Where hushed awakenings are dear...
But I've a rendezvous with Death
At midnight in some flaming town,
When Spring trips north again this year;
And I to my pledged word am true,
I shall not fail that rendezvous

THE LOVE SONG OF
J. ALFRED PRUFROCK

By
T. S. Eliot

T[homas] S[terns] Eliot (1888-1965) was an American-born writer, but is often thought of as a British writer because of his British citizenship (1927). He received a Bachelor of Arts and a Masters degree from Harvard. Later, Eliot studied at the Sorbonne and Oxford. His two most famous poems, "The Love Song of J. Alfred Prufrock" (1915) and The Waste Land (1922), set a different standard for modern poetry, which made Eliot a strong literary influence in the 20th century. Among his many awards are the Pulitzer Prize and the Nobel Prize for Literature (1948), received "for his outstanding pioneer contribution to present-day poetry." His poetry is highly allusive and complex. In addition to being a poet, he was a renowned playwright. After he converted to Anglicanism, Eliot's poetry took a decisively traditional turn in philosophy. Eliot died of emphysema in London at the age of 76.

> *S'io credesse che mia risposta fosse*
> *A persona che mai tornasse al mondo,*
> *Questa fiamma staria senza piu scosse.*
> *Ma perciocche giammai di questo fondo*
> *Non torno vivo alcun, s'i'odo il vero,*
> *Senza tema d'infamia ti rispondo.*[†]

Let us go then, you and I,
When the evening is spread out against the sky
Like a patient etherized upon a table;
Let us go, through certain half-deserted streets,
The muttering retreats
Of restless nights in one-night cheap hotels
And sawdust restaurants with oyster-shells:
Streets that follow like a tedious argument
Of insidious intent
To lead you to an overwhelming question...
Oh, do not ask, "What is it?"

Let us go and make our visit.
In the room the women come and go
Talking of Michelangelo.[†]

The yellow fog that rubs its back upon the window-panes,
The yellow smoke that rubs its muzzle on the window-panes,
Licked its tongue into the corners of the evening,
Lingered upon the pools that stand in drains,
Let fall upon its back the soot that falls from chimneys,
Slipped by the terrace, made a sudden leap,
And seeing that it was a soft October night,
Curled once about the house, and fell asleep.

And indeed there will be time
For the yellow smoke that slides along the street,
Rubbing its back upon the window-panes;
There will be time, there will be time
To prepare a face to meet the faces that you meet;
There will be time to murder and create,
And time for all the works and days of hands
That lift and drop a question on your plate;
Time for you and time for me,
And time yet for a hundred indecisions,
And for a hundred visions and revisions,
Before the taking of a toast and tea.

In the room the women come and go
Talking of Michelangelo.

And indeed there will be time
To wonder, "Do I dare?" and, "Do I dare?"
Time to turn back and descend the stair,
With a bald spot in the middle of my hair—
(They will say: "How his hair is growing thin!")
My morning coat, my collar mounting firmly to the chin,
My necktie rich and modest, but asserted by a simple pin—
(They will say: "But how his arms and legs are thin!")
Do I dare
Disturb the universe?
In a minute there is time
For decisions and revisions which a minute will reverse.

For I have known them all already, known them all:
Have known the evenings, mornings, afternoons,
I have measured out my life with coffee spoons;
I know the voices dying with a dying fall
Beneath the music from a farther room.
 So how should I presume?

And I have known the eyes already, known them all—
The eyes that fix you in a formulated phrase,
And when I am formulated, sprawling on a pin,
When I am pinned and wriggling on the wall,
Then how should I begin
To spit out all the butt-ends of my days and ways?
 And how should I presume?

And I have known the arms already, known them all—
Arms that are braceleted and white and bare
(But in the lamplight, downed with light brown hair!)
Is it perfume from a dress
That makes me so digress?
Arms that lie along a table, or wrap about a shawl.
 And should I then presume?
 And how should I begin?

Shall I say, I have gone at dusk through narrow streets
And watched the smoke that rises from the pipes
Of lonely men in shirt-sleeves, leaning out of windows?...

I should have been a pair of ragged claws
Scuttling across the floors of silent seas.

And the afternoon, the evening, sleeps so peacefully!
Smoothed by long fingers,
Asleep...tired...or it malingers,
Stretched on the floor, here beside you and me.
Should I, after tea and cakes and ices,
Have the strength to force the moment to its crisis?
But though I have wept and fasted, wept and prayed,
Though I have seen my head (grown slightly bald) brought in upon a
        platter,[†]
I am no prophet—and here's no great matter;
I have seen the moment of my greatness flicker,
And I have seen the eternal Footman[†] hold my coat, and snicker,
And in short, I was afraid.

And would it have been worth it, after all,
After the cups, the marmalade, the tea,
Among the porcelain, among some talk of you and me,
Would it have been worth while,
To have bitten off the matter with a smile,
To have squeezed the universe into a ball
To roll it toward some overwhelming question,
To say: "I am Lazarus,[†] come from the dead,
Come back to tell you all, I shall tell you all"—
If one, settling a pillow by her head
        Should say: "That is not what I meant at all;
        That is not it, at all."

And would it have been worth it, after all,
Would it have been worth while,
After the sunsets and the dooryards and the sprinkled streets,
After the novels, after the teacups, after the skirts that trail along the
        floor—
And this, and so much more?—
It is impossible to say just what I mean!
But as if a magic lantern[†] threw the nerves in patterns on a screen:
Would it have been worth while
If one, settling a pillow or throwing off a shawl,
And turning toward the window, should say:

"That is not it at all,
That is not what I meant, at all."

No! I am not Prince Hamlet,[†] nor was meant to be;
Am an attendant lord, one that will do
To swell a progress, start a scene or two,
Advise the prince; no doubt, an easy tool,
Deferential, glad to be of use,
Politic, cautious, and meticulous;
Full of high sentence, but a bit obtuse;
At times, indeed, almost ridiculous—
Almost, at times, the Fool.

I grow old...I grow old...
I shall wear the bottoms of my trousers rolled.

Shall I part my hair behind? Do I dare to eat a peach?
I shall wear white flannel trousers, and walk upon the beach.
I have heard the mermaids singing, each to each.

I do not think that they will sing to me.

I have seen them riding seaward on the waves
Combing the white hair of the waves blown back
When the wind blows the water white and black.
We have lingered in the chambers of the sea
By sea-girls wreathed with seaweed red and brown
Till human voices wake us, and we drown.

THE WASTE LAND

By
T. S. Eliot

"Nam Sibyllam quidem Cumis ego ipse oculis meis vidi in ampulla pen-
dere, et cum illi pueri dicerent: Σι′βυλλα τι′ θε′λεις; respondebat illa:
α′ποθανειν θε′λω."[†]

For Ezra Pound
il miglior fabbro.[†]

I. The Burial of the Dead

April is the cruellest month, breeding
Lilacs out of the dead land, mixing
Memory and desire, stirring
Dull roots with spring rain.
Winter kept us warm, covering
Earth in forgetful snow, feeding
A little life with dried tubers.
Summer surprised us, coming over the Starnbergersee[†]
With a shower of rain; we stopped in the colonnade,
And went on in sunlight, into the Hofgarten,[†]
And drank coffee, and talked for an hour.
Bin gar keine Russin, stamm' aus Litauen, echt deutsch.[†]
And when we were children, staying at the archduke's,[†]
My cousin's, he took me out on a sled,
And I was frightened. He said, Marie,
Marie,[†] hold on tight. And down we went.
In the mountains, there you feel free.
I read, much of the night, and go south in the winter.

What are the roots that clutch, what branches grow
Out of this stony rubbish? Son of man,[†]
You cannot say, or guess, for you know only
A heap of broken images, where the sun beats,
And the dead tree gives no shelter, the cricket no relief,
And the dry stone no sound of water. Only
There is shadow under this red rock,
(Come in under the shadow of this red rock),

And I will show you something different from either
Your shadow at morning striding behind you
Or your shadow at evening rising to meet you;
I will show you fear in a handful of dust.[†]

> *Frisch weht der Wind*
> *Der Heimat zu,*
> *Mein Irisch Kind,*
> *Wo weilest du?*[†]

"You gave me hyacinths first a year ago;
They called me the hyacinth girl."
—Yet when we came back, late, from the Hyacinth garden,
Your arms full, and your hair wet, I could not
Speak, and my eyes failed, I was neither
Living nor dead, and I knew nothing,
Looking into the heart of light, the silence.
Oed' und leer das Meer.[†]

Madame Sosostris, famous clairvoyante,
Had a bad cold, nevertheless
Is known to be the wisest woman in Europe,
With a wicked pack of cards.[†] Here, said she,
Is your card, the drowned Phoenician Sailor,
(Those are pearls that were his eyes. Look!)
Here is Belladonna,[†] the Lady of the Rocks,
The lady of situations.
Here is the man with three staves, and here the Wheel,
And here is the one-eyed merchant, and this card,
Which is blank, is something he carries on his back,
Which I am forbidden to see. I do not find
The Hanged Man.[†] Fear death by water.
I see crowds of people, walking round in a ring.
Thank you. If you see dear Mrs. Equitone,
Tell her I bring the horoscope myself:
One must be so careful these days.

Unreal City,[†]
Under the brown fog of a winter dawn,
A crowd flowed over London Bridge, so many,
I had not thought death had undone so many.[†]
Sighs, short and infrequent, were exhaled,[†]
And each man fixed his eyes before his feet.
Flowed up the hill and down King William Street,

To where Saint Mary Woolnoth[†] kept the hours
With a dead sound on the final stroke of nine.
There I saw one I knew, and stopped him, crying "Stetson!
"You who were with me in the ships at Mylae![†]
"That corpse you planted last year in your garden,[†]
"Has it begun to sprout? Will it bloom this year?
"Or has the sudden frost disturbed its bed?
"Oh keep the Dog far hence, that's friend to men,
"Or with his nails he'll dig it up again!
"You! hypocrite lecteur!—mon semblable,—mon frère![†]"

II. A Game of Chess

The Chair she sat in, like a burnished throne,
Glowed on the marble,[†] where the glass
Held up by standards wrought with fruited vines
From which a golden Cupidon peeped out
(Another hid his eyes behind his wing)
Doubled the flames of sevenbranched candelabra
Reflecting light upon the table as
The glitter of her jewels rose to meet it,
From satin cases poured in rich profusion;
In vials of ivory and coloured glass
Unstoppered, lurked her strange synthetic perfumes,
Unguent, powdered, or liquid—troubled, confused
And drowned the sense in odours; stirred by the air
That freshened from the window, these ascended
In fattening the prolonged candle-flames,
Flung their smoke into the laquearia,
Stirring the pattern on the coffered ceiling.
Huge sea-wood fed with copper
Burned green and orange, framed by the coloured stone,
In which sad light a carved dolphin swam.
Above the antique mantel was displayed
As though a window gave upon the sylvan scene
The change of Philomel, by the barbarous king
So rudely forced;[†] yet there the nightingale
Filled all the desert with inviolable voice
And still she cried, and still the world pursues,
"Jug Jug" to dirty ears.
And other withered stumps of time

Were told upon the walls; staring forms
Leaned out, leaning, hushing the room enclosed.
Footsteps shuffled on the stair.
Under the firelight, under the brush, her hair
Spread out in fiery points
Glowed into words, then would be savagely still.

"My nerves are bad to-night. Yes, bad. Stay with me.
"Speak to me. Why do you never speak. Speak.
        "What are you thinking of? What thinking? What?
"I never know what you are thinking. Think."

I think we are in rats' alley
Where the dead men lost their bones.

"What is that noise?"
                            The wind under the door.
"What is that noise now? What is the wind doing?"
                            Nothing again nothing.

                                                "Do
"You know nothing? Do you see nothing? Do you remember
Nothing?"
        I remember
Those are pearls that were his eyes.
"Are you alive, or not? Is there nothing in your head?"
                                                But

O O O O that Shakespeherian Rag†—
It's so elegant
So intelligent
"What shall I do now? What shall I do?"
"I shall rush out as I am, and walk the street
"With my hair down, so. What shall we do tomorrow?
"What shall we ever do?"
                            The hot water at ten.
And if it rains, a closed car at four.
And we shall play a game of chess,
Pressing lidless eyes and waiting for a knock upon the door.

When Lil's husband got demobbed, I said—
I didn't mince my words, I said to her myself,

HURRY UP PLEASE IT'S TIME[†]
Now Albert's coming back, make yourself a bit smart.
He'll want to know what you done with that money he gave you
To get yourself some teeth. He did, I was there.
You have them all out, Lil, and get a nice set,
He said, I swear, I can't bear to look at you.
And no more can't I, I said, and think of poor Albert,
He's been in the army four years, he wants a good time,
And if you don't give it him, there's others will, I said.
Oh is there, she said. Something o' that, I said.
Then I'll know who to thank, she said, and give me a straight look.
HURRY UP PLEASE IT'S TIME
If you don't like it you can get on with it, I said.
Others can pick and choose if you can't.
But if Albert makes off, it won't be for lack of telling.
You ought to be ashamed, I said, to look so antique.
(And her only thirty-one.)
I can't help it, she said, pulling a long face,
It's them pills I took, to bring it off, she said.
(She's had five already, and nearly died of young George.)
The chemist said it would be alright, but I've never been the same.
You are a proper fool, I said.
Well, if Albert won't leave you alone, there it is, I said,
What you get married for if you don't want children?
HURRY UP PLEASE IT'S TIME
Well, that Sunday Albert was home, they had a hot gammon,
And they asked me in to dinner, to get the beauty of it hot—
HURRY UP PLEASE IT'S TIME
HURRY UP PLEASE IT'S TIME
Goonight Bill. Goonight Lou. Goonight May. Goonight.
Ta ta. Goonight. Goonight.
Good night, ladies, good night, sweet ladies, good night, good night

III. The Fire Sermon[†]

The river's tent is broken: the last fingers of leaf
Clutch and sink into the wet bank. The wind
Crosses the brown land, unheard. The nymphs are departed.
Sweet Thames,[†] run softly, till I end my song.
The river bears no empty bottles, sandwich papers,
Silk handkerchiefs, cardboard boxes, cigarette ends

Or other testimony of summer nights. The nymphs are departed.
And their friends, the loitering heirs of city directors;
Departed, have left no addresses.
By the waters of Leman[†] I sat down and wept...
Sweet Thames, run softly till I end my song,
Sweet Thames, run softly, for I speak not loud or long.
But at my back in a cold blast I hear
The rattle of the bones, and chuckle spread from ear to ear.
A rat crept softly through the vegetation
Dragging its slimy belly on the bank
While I was fishing in the dull canal
On a winter evening round behind the gashouse
Musing upon the king my brother's wreck
And on the king my father's death before him.
White bodies naked on the low damp ground
And bones cast in a little low dry garret,
Rattled by the rat's foot only, year to year.
But at my back from time to time I hear
The sound of horns and motors, which shall bring
Sweeney to Mrs. Porter[†] in the spring.
O the moon shone bright on Mrs. Porter
And on her daughter
They wash their feet in soda water
Et, O ces voix d'enfants, chantant dans la coupole![†]

Twit twit twit
Jug jug jug jug jug jug
So rudely forc'd.
Tereu[†]

Unreal City
Under the brown fog of a winter noon
Mr. Eugenides, the Smyrna merchant
Unshaven, with a pocket full of currants
C.i.f. London: documents at sight,
Asked me in demotic French
To luncheon at the Cannon Street Hotel
Followed by a weekend at the Metropole.[†]

At the violet hour, when the eyes and back
Turn upward from the desk, when the human engine waits
Like a taxi throbbing waiting,

I Tiresias,[†] though blind, throbbing between two lives,
Old man with wrinkled female breasts, can see
At the violet hour, the evening hour that strives
Homeward, and brings the sailor home from sea,
The typist home at teatime, clears her breakfast, lights
Her stove, and lays out food in tins.
Out of the window perilously spread
Her drying combinations touched by the sun's last rays,
On the divan are piled (at night her bed)
Stockings, slippers, camisoles, and stays.
I Tiresias, old man with wrinkled dugs
Perceived the scene, and foretold the rest—
I too awaited the expected guest.
He, the young man carbuncular, arrives,
A small house agent's clerk, with one bold stare,
One of the low on whom assurance sits
As a silk hat on a Bradford millionaire.
The time is now propitious, as he guesses,
The meal is ended, she is bored and tired,
Endeavours to engage her in caresses
Which still are unreproved, if undesired.
Flushed and decided, he assaults at once;
Exploring hands encounter no defence;
His vanity requires no response,
And makes a welcome of indifference.
(And I Tiresias have foresuffered all
Enacted on this same divan or bed;
I who have sat by Thebes below the wall
And walked among the lowest of the dead.)
Bestows one final patronising kiss,
And gropes his way, finding the stairs unlit...

She turns and looks a moment in the glass,
Hardly aware of her departed lover;
Her brain allows one half-formed thought to pass:
"Well now that's done: and I'm glad it's over."
When lovely woman stoops to folly and
Paces about her room again, alone,
She smoothes her hair with automatic hand,
And puts a record on the gramophone.

"This music crept by me upon the waters"
And along the Strand, up Queen Victoria Street.
O City city, I can sometimes hear
Beside a public bar in Lower Thames Street,
The pleasant whining of a mandoline
And a clatter and a chatter from within
Where fishmen lounge at noon: where the walls
Of Magnus Martyr[†] hold
Inexplicable splendour of Ionian white and gold.

>   The river sweats
>   Oil and tar
>   The barges drift
>   With the turning tide
>   Red sails
>   Wide
>   To leeward, swing on the heavy spar.
>   The barges wash
>   Drifting logs
>   Down Greenwich[†] reach
>   Past the Isle of Dogs.[†]
>   Weialala leia[†]
>   Wallala leialala

>   Elizabeth and Leicester[†]
>   Beating oars
>   The stern was formed
>   A gilded shell
>   Red and gold
>   The brisk swell
>   Rippled both shores
>   Southwest wind
>   Carried down stream
>   The peal of bells
>   White towers
>   Weialala leia
>   Wallala leialala

"Trams and dusty trees.
Highbury bore me. Richmond and Kew[†]
Undid me. By Richmond I raised my knees
Supine on the floor of a narrow canoe."

"My feet are at Moorgate, and my heart
Under my feet. After the event
He wept. He promised 'a new start.'
I made no comment. What should I resent?"

"On Margate Sands.[†]
I can connect
Nothing with nothing.
The broken fingernails of dirty hands.
My people humble people who expect
Nothing."
              la la

To Carthage then I came[†]

Burning burning burning burning
O Lord Thou pluckest me out
O Lord Thou pluckest

burning

IV. Death By Water

Phlebas the Phoenician, a fortnight dead,
Forgot the cry of gulls, and the deep sea swell
And the profit and loss.
                    A current under sea
Picked his bones in whispers. As he rose and fell
He passed the stages of his age and youth
Entering the whirlpool.
                 Gentile or Jew
O you who turn the wheel and look to windward,
Consider Phlebas, who was once handsome and tall as you.

V. What the Thunder Said

After the torchlight red on sweaty faces
After the frosty silence in the gardens
After the agony in stony places
The shouting and the crying

Prison and palace and reverberation
Of thunder of spring over distant mountains
He who was living is now dead
We who were living are now dying
With a little patience

Here is no water but only rock
Rock and no water and the sandy road
The road winding above among the mountains
Which are mountains of rock without water
If there were water we should stop and drink
Amongst the rock one cannot stop or think
Sweat is dry and feet are in the sand
If there were only water amongst the rock
Dead mountain mouth of carious teeth that cannot spit
Here one can neither stand nor lie nor sit
There is not even silence in the mountains
But dry sterile thunder without rain
There is not even solitude in the mountains
But red sullen faces sneer and snarl
From doors of mudcracked houses

                              If there were water

   And no rock
   If there were rock
   And also water[†]
   And water
   A spring
   A pool among the rock
   If there were the sound of water only
   Not the cicada
   And dry grass singing
   But sound of water over a rock
   Where the hermit-thrush sings in the pine trees
   Drip drop drip drop drop drop drop
   But there is no water

Who is the third who walks always beside you?[†]
When I count, there are only you and I together
But when I look ahead up the white road
There is always another one walking beside you
Gliding wrapt in a brown mantle, hooded
I do not know whether a man or a woman
—But who is that on the other side of you?

What is that sound high in the air
Murmur of maternal lamentation
Who are those hooded hordes swarming
Over endless plains, stumbling in cracked earth
Ringed by the flat horizon only
What is the city over the mountains
Cracks and reforms and bursts in the violet air
Falling towers
Jerusalem Athens Alexandria
Vienna London
Unreal

A woman drew her long black hair out tight
And fiddled whisper music on those strings
And bats with baby faces in the violet light
Whistled, and beat their wings
And crawled head downward down a blackened wall
And upside down in air were towers
Tolling reminiscent bells, that kept the hours
And voices singing out of empty cisterns and exhausted wells.

In this decayed hole among the mountains
In the faint moonlight, the grass is singing
Over the tumbled graves, about the chapel
There is the empty chapel, only the wind's home.
It has no windows, and the door swings,
Dry bones can harm no one.
Only a cock stood on the rooftree
Co co rico co co rico[†]
In a flash of lightning. Then a damp gust
Bringing rain

Ganga[†] was sunken, and the limp leaves
Waited for rain, while the black clouds
Gathered far distant, over Himavant.[†]
The jungle crouched, humped in silence.
Then spoke the thunder
DA
Datta:[†] what have we given?
My friend, blood shaking my heart
The awful daring of a moment's surrender
Which an age of prudence can never retract

By this, and this only, we have existed
Which is not to be found in our obituaries
Or in memories draped by the beneficent spider
Or under seals broken by the lean solicitor
In our empty rooms
DA
Dayadhvam:[†] I have heard the key
Turn in the door once and turn once only
We think of the key, each in his prison
Thinking of the key, each confirms a prison
Only at nightfall, aethereal rumours
Revive for a moment a broken Coriolanus[†]
DA
Damyata:[†] The boat responded
Gaily, to the hand expert with sail and oar
The sea was calm, your heart would have responded
Gaily, when invited, beating obedient
To controlling hands

                                   I sat upon the shore
Fishing, with the arid plain behind me
Shall I at least set my lands in order?
London Bridge is falling down falling down falling down
Poi s'ascose nel foco che gli affina[†]
Quando fiam uti chelidon[†]—O swallow swallow
Le Prince d'Aquitaine à la tour abolie[†]
These fragments I have shored against my ruins
Why then Ile fit you. Hieronymo's mad againe.[†]
Datta. Dayadhvam. Damyata.
        Shantih shantih shantih[†]

When the Year Grows Old

By

Edna St. Vincent Millay

Edna St. Vincent Millay (1892-1950) mixed traditional verse with modern content in her poetry, particularly in her sonnets. In 1917, after graduating from Vassar, Millay chose a bohemian lifestyle, living Greenwich Village. Critics recognized her early as a poet with promise when, at 20 years old, she published "Renascence," which won a poetry contest. Millay presented her poetry in various readings throughout the world. A heart attack claimed her when she was 58 years old.

When the year grows old—
October—November—
How she disliked the cold!

She used to watch the swallows
Go down across the sky,
And turn from the window
With a little sharp sigh.

And often when the brown leaves
Were brittle on the ground,
And the wind in the chimney
Made a melancholy sound,

She had a look about her
That I wish I could forget—
The look of a scared thing
Sitting in a net!

Oh, beautiful at nightfall
The soft spitting snow!
And beautiful the bare boughs
Rubbing to and fro!

But the roaring of the fire,
And the warmth of fur,
And the boiling of the kettle
Were beautiful to her!

I cannot but remember
When the year grows old—
October—November—
How she disliked the cold!

BUFFALO BILL'S †

By

E. E. Cummings

E[dward] E[stin] Cummings (1894-1962) was born in Cambridge, Massachusetts. By 1904, he had begun writing poetry, and his first published poems appeared in an anthology, Eight Harvard Poets, in 1917. He earned both a Bachelors and Masters degree from Harvard. After service as an ambulance driver in World War I, Cummings lived in Connecticut and Greenwich Village and often traveled to Europe. Cummings is known for his non-traditional use of punctuation, spelling, and syntax, his lack of concern about margins on the page, and the simplicity of his language. Much of his poetic style seems to imitate the rhythms of jazz. When he began his career, he wrote his name in all lowercase letters, but altered it to the more traditional form in the 1930s. E.E. Cummings died of a cerebral hemorrhage at the age of 68, leaving behind over 25 books of prose, poetry, drawings, plays, and stories

Buffalo Bill's
defunct
     who used to
     ride a watersmooth-silver

               stallion
and break onetwothreefourfive pigeonsjustlikethat
                     Jesus
he was a handsome man
          and what i want to know is
how do you like your blueeyed boy
Mister Death

IN JUST-

By
E. E. Cummings

in Just-
spring   when the world is mud-
luscious the little
lame balloonman

whistles far   and wee

and eddyandbill come
running from marbles and
piracies and it's
spring

when the world is puddle-wonderful

the queer
old balloonman whistles
far   and   wee
and bettyandisabel come dancing

from hop-scotch and jump-rope and

it's
spring
and
         the
goat-footed

balloonMan   whistles
far
and
wee

HER LIPS ARE COPPER WIRE

By
Jean Toomer

Jean Toomer [Nathan Pinchback Toomer] (1894-1967) is often associated with ideals of the Lost Generation of Hemingway and the Harlem Renaissance. He was a complex man who, although African-American, often passed for white. Toomer was born in Washington, D. C. He spent his academic life in at least six colleges and universities in a number of majors, but never earned a degree. His desire was to be a writer, so he prepared himself by listening to lectures, reading the great writers, and joining various literary groups. Strongly philosophical in his works, he wrote in several genres—poetry, short story, drama, and essay. Toomer died in Doylestown, Pennsylvania, in 1967

whisper of yellow globes
gleaming on lamp-posts that sway
like bootleg licker drinkers in the fog

and let your breath be moist against me
like bright beads on yellow globes

telephone the power-house
that the main wires are insulate

(her words play softly up and down
dewy corridors of billboards)

then with your tongue remove the tape
and press your lips to mine
till they are incandescent

PORTRAIT OF A BOY

By
Stephen Vincent Benét

After the whipping he crawled into bed,
Accepting the harsh fact with no great weeping.
How funny uncle's hat had looked striped red!
He chuckled silently. The moon came, sweeping
A black, frayed rag of tattered cloud before
In scorning; very pure and pale she seemed,
Flooding his bed with radiance. On the floor
Fat motes danced. He sobbed, closed his eyes and dreamed.

Warm sand flowed round him. Blurts of crimson light
Splashed the white grains like blood. Past the cave's mouth
Shone with a large, fierce splendor, wildly bright,
The crooked constellations of the South;
Here the Cross† swung; and there, affronting Mars,
The Centaur† stormed aside a froth of stars.
Within, great casks, like wattled aldermen,
Sighed of enormous feasts, and cloth of gold
Glowed on the walls like hot desire. Again,
Beside webbed purples from some galleon's hold,
A black chest bore the skull and bones in white
Above a scrawled "Gunpowder!" By the flames,
Decked out in crimson, gemmed with syenite,
Hailing their fellows with outrageous names,
The pirates sat and diced. Their eyes were moons.
"Doubloons!" they said. The words crashed gold. "Doubloons!"

H A R L E M   (2)

By
Langston Hughes

Langston Hughes (1902-1967) was part of the Harlem Renaissance. He was born in Joplin, Missouri, but after his parents divorced, was raised by his maternal grandmother while his mother worked. Hughes lived in Kansas, Illinois, and Ohio as a youth. In 1921, he attended Columbia University, studying engineering, but left because of racism there. Later, at Lincoln University, he earned a Bachelor of Arts degree (1929) then a Doctor of Letters (1943). As an adult, Hughes traveled widely and worked blue-collar jobs so that he could write. His first and most famous work is The Weary Blues (1926), which contains the poem, "The Negro Speaks of Rivers." Hughes expressed his views in a variety of genres, including poems, novels, plays, and short stories. He succumbed to prostate cancer at the age of 65

What happens to a dream deferred?

Does it dry up
like a raisin in the sun?
Or fester like a sore—
And then run?
Does it stink like rotten meat?
Or crust and sugar over
like a syrupy sweet?

Maybe it just sags
like a heavy load.

Or does it explode?

POET TO BIGOT

By
Langston Hughes

I have done so little
For you,
And you have done so little
For me,
That we have good reason
Never to agree.

I, however,
Have such meagre
Power,
Clutching at a
Moment,
While you control
An hour.

But your hour is
A stone.

My Moment is
A flower.

The Negro Speaks of Rivers

By
Langston Hughes

I've known rivers:
I've known rivers ancient as the world and older than the flow of human
blood in human veins.

My soul has grown deep like the rivers.

I bathed in the Euphrates[†] when dawns were young.
I build my hut near the Congo[†] and it lulled me to sleep.
I looked upon the Nile[†] and raised the pyramids above it.
I heard the singing of the Mississippi[†] when Abe Lincoln went down to
New Orleans, [†] and I've seen its muddy bosom turn all golden in
the sunset.

I've known rivers:
Ancient, dusky rivers.

My soul has grown deep like the rivers.

MY DREAMS, MY WORKS, MUST WAIT TILL AFTER HELL

By
Gwendolyn Brooks

Gwendolyn Brooks (1917-2000) was born in Topeka, Kansas, and raised in Chicago, Illinois, where she lived until her death. At 13, Brooks had a poem published in a children's magazine, and by 17, more were published. Brooks authored more than 20 books of poetry, beginning with A Street in Bronzeville *(1945), which brought her both popular and critical recognition. Brooks received the Pulitzer Prize in poetry for* Annie Allen *(1949), the first African-American recipient of a Pulitzer. In 1968, Brooks was named the Poet Laureate of Illinois, following Carl Sandburg; she was also the Consultant in Poetry to the Library of Congress from 1985-1986.*

I hold my honey and I store my bread
In little jars and cabinets of my will.
I label clearly, and each latch and lid
I bid, Be firm till I return from hell.
I am very hungry. I am incomplete.
And none can give me any word but Wait,
The puny light. I keep my eyes pointed in;
Hoping that, when the devil days of my hurt

Drag out to their last dregs and I resume
On such legs as are left me, in such heart
As I can manage, remember to go home,
My taste will not have turned insensitive
To honey and bread old purity could love.

A SUPERMARKET IN CALIFORNIA

By

Allen Ginsberg

Allen Ginsberg (1926-1997) was a modern poet who was active in the Beat Movement of the 1960s. Ginsberg's Jewish parents had a strong in influence on him. His mother often took him to Communist Party meetings, and his father was himself a poet. Ginsberg lived in Paterson, New Jersey, as a child. He attended Columbia University and was active in several literary activities there. In his later years, Ginsberg traveled the world and studied Buddhism, Zen, and Krishnaism. His controversial poem, "Howl" (1956), decries the traditional values and the materialism of modern America, while praising his non-conformist friends of the Beat Generation. He later became a spokesman against the Vietnam War and for gay rights. Ginsberg died of liver cancer at the age of 70.

What thoughts I have of you tonight, Walt Whitman,[†] for I walked down the sidestreets under the trees with a headache self-conscious looking at the full moon.
In my hungry fatigue, and shopping for images, I went into the neon fruit supermarket, dreaming of your enumerations!
What peaches and what penumbras! Whole families shopping at night! Aisles full of husbands! Wives in the avocados, babies in the tomatoes!— and you, Garcia Lorca,[†] what
were you doing down by the watermelons?

I saw you, Walt Whitman, childless, lonely old grubber, poking among the
meats in the refrigerator and eyeing the grocery boys.
I heard you asking questions of each: Who killed the pork chops? What
price bananas? Are you my Angel?
I wandered in and out of the brilliant stacks of cans following you, and followed in my imagination by the store detective.
We strode down the open corridors together in our solitary fancy tasting
artichokes, possessing every frozen delicacy, and never passing the cashier.

Where are we going, Walt Whitman? The doors close in an hour. Which
way does your beard point tonight?
(I touch your book and dream of our odyssey in the supermarket and feel
absurd.)
Will we walk all night through solitary streets? The trees add shade to
shade, lights out in the houses, we'll both be lonely.

Will we stroll dreaming of the lost America of love past blue automobiles
in driveways, home to our silent cottage? Ah, dear father, graybeard, lonely
old courage-teacher,
what America did you have when Charon[†] quit poling his ferry and you
got out on a smoking bank and stood watching the boat disappear on the
black waters of Lethe?[†]

THE WHISTLE

By

Yusef Komunyakaa

Yusef Komunyakaa (b.1947) was born and raised in Bogalusa, Louisiana, during the beginning of the Civil Rights Movement. He received a Bronze Star for serving in the United States Army during the Vietnam War. He earned undergraduate and graduate degrees from universities in Colorado and California. Komunyakaa has published ten books of poems since 1977. In addition, he has co-edited anthologies, written dramatic works and a libretto. He has received numerous literary awards, including the Pulitzer Prize in 1994 for Neon Vernacular: New & Selected Poems 1977-1989. *Currently, he resides in New York City and is the Distinguished Senior Poet in NYU's graduate creative writing program.*

The seven o'clock whistle
Made the morning air fulvous
With a metallic syncopation,
A key to a door in the sky—opening
& closing flesh. The melody
Men & women built lives around,
Sonorous as the queen bee's fat
Hum drawing workers from flowers,
Back to the colonized heart.
A titanous puff of steam rose
From the dragon trapped below
Iron, bricks, & wood.

The whole black machine
Shuddered: blue jays & redbirds
Wove light through leaves
& something dead under the foundation
Brought worms to life.
Men capped their thermoses,
Switched off Loretta Lynn,[†]
& slid from trucks & cars.
The rip saws throttled
& swung out over logs
On conveyer belts.
Daddy lifted the tongs
To his right shoulder…a winch
Uncoiled the steel cable
From its oily scrotum;
He waved to the winchman
& iron teeth bit into the pine.
Yellow forklifts darted
With lumber to boxcars
Marked for distant cities.
At noon, Daddy would walk
Across the field of goldenrod
& mustard weeds, the pollen
Bright & sullen on his overalls.
He'd eat on our screened-in
Back porch—red beans & rice
With hamhocks & cornbread.
Lemonade & peach Jello.

The one o'clock bleat
Burned sweat & salt into afternoon
& the wheels within wheels
Unlocked again, pulling rough boards
Into the plane's pneumatic grip.
Wild geese moved like a wedge
Between sky & sagebrush,
As Daddy pulled the cable
To the edge of the millpond
& sleepwalked cypress logs.
The day turned on its axle
& pyramids of russet sawdust
Formed under corrugated
Blowpipes fifty feet high.
The five o'clock whistle
Bellowed like a bull, controlling
Clocks on kitchen walls;
Women dabbed loud perfume
Behind their ears & set tables
Covered with flowered oilcloth.

8 FRAGMENTS FOR KURT COBAIN

By
Jim Carroll

Jim Carroll (b.1951), born on August 8, 1951, in New York City, is known primarily as a talented poet and musician. Though he suffered through a period of drug addiction in his early teens, he wrote and published his first book, Organic Trains, *when he was only 16.* The Basketball Diaries: Age Twelve to Fifteen, *which was published to great acclaim, also became a 1995 movie. In addition, Carroll appeared in an MTV Unplugged session in 1994 and read "8 Fragments for Kurt Cobain," the poem that appears in this anthology.*

1/
Genius is not a generous thing
In return it charges more interest than any amount of royalties can cover
And it resents fame
With bitter vengeance
Pills and powders† only placate it awhile
Then it puts you in a place where the planet's poles reverse
Where the currents of electricity shift
Your Body becomes a magnet and pulls to it despair and rotten teeth,
Cheese whiz and guns
Whose triggers are shaped tenderly into a false lust
In timeless illusion

2/

The guitar claws kept tightening, I guess on your heart stem.
The loops of feedback and distortion, threaded right thru
Lucifer's[†] wisdom teeth, and never stopped their reverberating
In your mind
And from the stage
All the faces out front seemed so hungry
With an unbearably wholesome misunderstanding
From where they sat, you seemed so far up there
High and live and diving
And instead you were swamp crawling
Down, deeper
Until you tasted the Earth's own blood
And chatted with the Buzzing-eyed insects that heroin breeds

3/

You should have talked more with the monkey[†]
He's always willing to negotiate
I'm still paying him off...
The greater the money and fame
The slower the Pendulum of fortune swings
Your will could have sped it up...
But you left that in a plane
Because it wouldn't pass customs and immigration

4/

Here's synchronicity for you:
Your music's tape was inside my walkman
When my best friend from summer camp
Called with the news about you
I listened then...
It was all there!
Your music kept cutting deeper and deeper valleys of sound
Less and less light
Until you hit solid rock
The drill bit broke
and the valley became
A thin crevice, impassible in time,
As time itself stopped.
And the walls became cages of brilliant notes
Pressing in...
Pressure
That's how diamonds are made
And that's WHERE it sometimes all collapses
Down in on you

5/

Then I translated your muttered lyrics
And the phrases were curious:
Like "incognito libido"
And "Chalk Skin Bending"
The words kept getting smaller and smaller
Until
Separated from their music
Each letter spilled out into a cartridge
Which fit only in the barrel of a gun

6/

And you shoved the barrel in as far as possible
Because that's where the pain came from
That's where the demons were digging
The world outside was blank
Its every cause was just a continuation
Of another unsolved effect

7/

But Kurt...
Didn't the thought that you would never write another song
Another feverish line or riff
Make you think twice?
That's what I don't understand
Because it's kept me alive, above any wounds

8/

If only you hadn't swallowed yourself into a coma in Roma[†]...
You could have gone to Florence
And looked into the eyes of Bellini or Rafael's Portraits[†]
Perhaps inside them
You could have found a threshold back to beauty's arms
Where it all began...
No matter that you felt betrayed by her
That is always the cost
As Frank said,
Of a young artist's remorseless passion
Which starts out as a kiss
And follows like a curse

Glossary

Upon A Wasp Chilled With Cold
The bear...northern blast – an allusion to an Iroquois Indian legend that relates that a bear's breath can freeze waters; therefore, the bear was given the task of being in charge of the winter winds
Sol's – the sun's
Did turret rationality – As if the wasp's movements indicate intelligence
whereof thou up dost hasp – "which you (God) has given"
pipes – another word for voice

An Hymn to the Evening
Aurora – the Roman goddess of the dawn

The Star-Spangled Banner
O'er – Over

A Visit from St. Nicholas
like the down of a thistle – The seed of a thistle (a purple weed) appears soft and fluffy and easily blows away with a breath of air.

Thanatopsis
last bitter hour – the time of death
narrow house – the coffin or grave
patriarchs of the infant world – the early Hebrews before written records
Barcan wilderness – a desolate area in North Africa
Oregon – a river in northwest United States

Paul Revere's Ride
North Church – a famous Bostonian church, built in 1723
Middlesex — the Massachusetts county where Boston was founded; it was named for a county in England.
Charlestown – a Colonial town north of Boston, situated between the Mystic and Charles Rivers
Mystic – a river near Boston
Lexington – the famous site of the first shots fired during the Revolutionary War, seven miles from Boston
Concord town – a small Colonial town nineteen miles northeast of Boston
ball for ball – literally, "shot for shot"; early ammunition was shaped into small lead balls.

The Children's Hour

Alice, Allegra, Edith – the names of Longfellow's three daughters

Bishop of Bingen – the ruler of a district on the Rhine River near Cologne, Germany

Mouse-Tower on the Rhine – a reference to a German folktale, in which the mice and rats eat all of the Bishop's stored food

The Village Blacksmith

chaff from a threshing-floor – the waste left from grains that remains on the floor

The Wreck of the Hesperus

fairy-flax – a blue flower

Spanish Main – an area along the northern coast of South America; the Caribbean and nearby waters; the merchant trip from America to Europe

smote amain – struck the middle of

Christ, who…Lake of Galilee – a reference to the Biblical account in Luke 8:22-25, in which Christ calmed a storm

Norman's Woe – a rocky area off the east coast of Cape Anne, Massachusetts, known for numerous shipwrecks

carded wool – wool that has been straightened by brushing with a carder to prepare it for spinning into thread

Barbara Frietchie

Frederick – a town in Maryland, which was a crossroads to the North during the Revolutionary and Civil Wars

Lee – Robert E. Lee, the general of the Confederate Army

fourscore years and ten – 90 years old

Stonewall Jackson – a famous southern general

Rebel – a reference to Stonewall Jackson

Annabel Lee

Annabel Lee – assumed to be Poe's young wife, Virginia Clemm

seraphs in heaven – the highest order of God's angels

high-born kinsmen – angels, seraphs

The Bells

Runic rhyme – a mysterious type of writing using symbols instead of letters

The Raven

volume of forgotten lore – a book of learning

ember – burning wood in the fireplace

bust of Pallas – a sculpture of Athena, the Greek goddess of wisdom

Night's Plutonian shore – a reference to the Underworld in Roman mythology

perfumed from an unseen censer – odor from the burning of incense

Seraphim –types of angels described in the Bible that have six wings and exist around the throne of God in heaven

nepenthe – a drink that makes one forget

Tempter – Satan, the devil

balm in Gilead – a Biblical allusion meaning something to give comfort to

distant Aidenn – a Biblical allusion to the Garden of Eden

To Helen

Helen – Helen of Troy from Greek mythology, who was considered the most beautiful woman in the world

Nicean barks of yore – an allusion to Nicea, a city near Troy in Greek mythology; old ships from Nicea

wanderer – Ulysses

hyacinth – a reference to Hyacinthus, a male Greek mythological hero, beloved but accidentally killed by Apollo; also a flower

Naiad airs – The Naiads were Greek goddesses who reigned over water; "airs" refers to the "songs" and sounds that water makes

Psyche – the beautiful princess in mythology who eventually married Cupid

Holy-Land – Greece and Rome

Old Ironsides

Her deck, …heroes' blood – an allusion to the past battles in which Old Ironsides fought

harpies – Greek spirits with claws, beaks, and wings, who would punish and harass people

The Chambered Nautilus

Siren – three bird-like women in Greek mythology who seduce ships into shipwreck by their singing

Triton blew from wreathèd horn – the son of Poseidon, half man and half fish, who comes to the surface to blow his horn, which is similar to the spiral shape of the nautilus

I Knew A Man By Sight

——

Gettysburg

the ark of our holy cause – a reference to the Ark of the Covenant, a physical symbol of God, kept and worshipped by the Israelites as they traveled through the desert

Dagon – an Old Testament pagan idol that fell on its face before the Ark of the Covenant (I Samuel 5:2-7)

warrior-monument – a statue on Cemetery Ridge at Gettysburg that was damaged by Southern forces

from Song of Myself

plumb in the uprights – a construction or contracting term meaning something is perfectly vertical

Kanuck – a slang term for a French Canadian

Tuckahoe – a Native American

Cuff – a mean person

I Hear America Singing

——

O Captain! My Captain!

Captain – Abraham Lincoln; President of the United States, assassinated at the end of the Civil War

ship – the Union; the United States of America

When I Heard the Learn'd Astronomer

——

The Battle Hymn of the Republic

Hero, born of woman – a reference to Christ

crush the serpent with his heel – a Biblical allusion to Genesis 3:15, meaning the final victory of Christ over Satan (the serpent)

Because I could not stop for Death

——

Hope is the thing with Feathers

——

<u>I can wade grief</u>
Himmaleh – the Himalayan Mountains

<u>I died for beauty</u>
——

<u>I heard a fly buzz when I died</u>
king – a symbolic use for the word *death*
windows – eyes

<u>I never saw a moor</u>
——

<u>I'm nobody! Who are you?</u>
——

<u>Success is Counted Sweetest</u>
——

<u>Romeo and Juliet</u>
——

<u>A Morning Fancy</u>
——

<u>The New Colossus</u>
The New Colossus – a reference to the Colossus of Rhodes, a statue built
    on the island of Rhodes, and one of the Seven Wonders of the World
giant of Greek fame – the Colossus of Rhodes
mighty woman with a torch – the Statue of Liberty, given to the United
    States by France in 1886
The air-bridged...cities frame – The Brooklyn Bridge, completed in 1883,
    connected what were then the two separate cities of Brooklyn and New
    York.
ancient lands – the Old World, particularly Europe
storied pomp – the grand tales of the Old World
golden door – the United States, the land of opportunity

<u>A Caged Bird</u>
——

The Bumblebee
fagged-out – tired
hollyhawks – hollyhocks (flowers)
jimson-blossom – a jimson-weed, a poisonous plant with trumpet-shaped
    flowers
Raggedy Man – hired help, a farmhand
muntain – maintain

When the Frost is on the Punkin
fodder's – corn stalks harvested for feed
shock – corn gathered together to dry
kyouck, gobble, clackin', cluckin' – the onomatopoetic sounds of the farm
    animal
airly – early
husky, rusty...the corn – the sounds of the dried corn sheaves
furries – furrows
medder – meadow
hosses – horses
clover over-head – Dried clover makes hay, whish is stored in the upper
    part of the barn.
poured around the celler-floor – Farmers stored apples for winter in the
    cold earth of the cellar.
souse and saussage – Butchering and canning was done in the fall.

Solitude

In War-Time (An American Homeward-Bound)
Fates – the three Greek goddesses who determined man's destiny

Tears
Homer his sight – a reference to the famous blind poet of ancient Greece
David his little lad – King David of Israel, who, when young, killed the
    giant Goliath

America the Beautiful
amber waves of grain – the golden color of the wheat fields
sea to shining sea – from the Atlantic ocean to the Pacific ocean

Casey at the Bat
With the hope...the human breast – a quotation by Alexander Pope from
    An Essay on Man (1733)

When Ol' Sis' Judy Pray

Mount Sin-a-i – the mountain where Moses received the Ten
Commandments, found in (Exodus 19)
Debbil tu'n – the Devil turns
sinnahs – sinners
sinnahs trimble – sinners tremble
Ter hyuh huh voice in sorro 'peat – "To hear her voice in sorrow repeat"
Dat melt all...ur stone – "that melt all hearts though made of stone"
An' hebben on de Yurf am foun' – "And heaven on the earth is found"
Jahsper – a reference to Revelation 21, where the walls of heaven are made
of a red-colored gem, jasper

Aner Clute

——

Hod Putt

——

Homer Clapp

——

The Hill

hill – the cemetery in Spoon River, Illinois

A Litany of Atlanta

Hear us, good Lord! – Many of the lines in the poem either are direct
quotations or paraphrases from the Bible.
Jehovah jireh – a reference to the Book of Genesis; it means, "The Lord
will provide."
Selah! – This word has no exact meaning. It is intended as a pause or
response.
In yonder East...star – a reference to the star of Bethlehem
Kyrie Eleison! – Greek for "Lord, have mercy"

Miniver Cheevy

Thebes – an important Greek city, also the ancient capital city of Egypt
Camelot – the magical English city of King Arthur
Priam's – the mythological king of Troy
Medici – a powerful Italian family that ruled from the 1200s -1660s
khaki suit – the clothing of a soldier
iron clothing – knight's armor

Richard Cory
––––

A man adrift on a slim spar
the hollow of The Hand – a Biblical expression that means God can hold
all the oceans in the hollow of His hand (Isaiah 40:12)

A man said: "Thou tree!"
––––

I stood upon a high place
––––

In the desert
––––

Should the wide world roll away
––––

from War Is Kind

affrighted steed – frightened horse

Lift Ev'ry Voice and Sing
This poem is sometimes referred to as "The Black National Anthem."

The Creation
God scooped the clay – God created man from the dust of the earth
(Genesis 2:7)
he shaped it in…blew the breath of life – a Biblical reference from
Genesis that says that God made man in His own image and breathed
into him the breath of life

Misapprehension
––––

We Wear the Mask
––––

Harvest Moon
––––

Harvest Moon: 1916
Light of Light – a reference to Jesus Christ

Madonna of the Evening Flowers
Canterbury bells – small flowers shaped like bells
pyrus japonica – a type of small shrub
Te Deums of the Canterbury bells – an anthem or hymn of praise to God, often repeated in a service

The Cyclists
The Dominant Mother – England, once a country of great power

The Cremation of Sam McGee
Northern Lights – an astronomical phenomena, of colored lights in the sky; they are found around the Northern polar regions, and are called the aurora borealis.
Lake Lebarge – a large lake at the end of the Yukon River in the Arctic
Dawson trail – the road between Whitehorse and Dawson City in the Yukon

The Death of the Hired Man
hazel prong – a forked piece of wood used to find water under the ground

Fire and Ice
——

The Road Not Taken
——

Two Tramps in Mud Time

playing possum – pretending
witching-wand – a forked piece of wood used as a divining rod to find water

I Sit and Sew
writhing grotesque things – wounded and hurt men

Grandmither, think not I forget
mayhap – maybe, perhaps
gie – give
'twixt sundown an' the dawn! – between sundown and the dawn

Chicago

Hog Butcher for the World – Chicago was the meat packing center of the United States from the mid 19th Century to the late 20th Century

painted women – prostitutes

Chicago Poet

Fog

Grass

Austerlitz, Waterloo, Gettysburg, Ypres, Verdun – battles from 1805 to 1916 in Europe and America that resulted in huge loss of life on the battlefields

Shenandoah

Shenandoah Valley – an area in Virginia that served the main food production source for the Confederacy

one rider gray and one rider blue – Soldiers in the Civil War wore blue uniforms (North) or gray uniforms (South).

Smoke

General Booth Enters Into Heaven

William Booth – (1829-1912), the founder of the Salvation Army in England

Are you washed...the Lamb? – a popular hymn sung by the Salvation Army to draw sinners to Christ

half-a-score – ten

banjos bang – a popular string instrument, used by the members of the Salvation Army to attract attention to gather crowds for their street meetings

The Emperor of Ice-Cream

dresser of deal – a small wooden cabinet

Let Me Live Out My Years

Thing – death

The Red Wheelbarrow
――

This Is Just to Say
――

I Shall Not Care
――

The Kiss
――

The Proud Poet
Shaemas O'Sheel – (1886-1954), an Irish-American poet
Byron...to fight against the Turk – George Gordon Byron or Lord Byron (1788-1824), a popular British Romantic poet who traveled widely in Europe, eventually joining the fight for Greek independence against the Turks.
David, the Singing King of the Jews – the king of Israel, known for singing to King Solomon and writing most of the Psalms in the Bible
Rupert Brooke – (1887-1915), a British poet, known for his poem "The Soldier"; he died during World War I.
Sir Philip Sidney's – (1554-1586), an Elizabethan soldier and poet who wrote *Astrophel and Stella*
Sir Walter Raleigh – (1552-1618), an Elizabethan adventurer and writer of poetry and history: he was beheaded by Queen Elizabeth I.
Homer – the blind Greek poet who wrote *The Iliad* and *The Odyssey*
Heine – Heinrich Heine (1779-1856), a German Romantic poet
Prometheus, torn...is never done – the Greek mythological hero who stole fire and gave it to mankind; his punishment was to have his liver eaten away by an eagle every day, only to have it grow back each night.

Trees
――

Oread
――

I Have a Rendezvous with Death
――

The Love Song of J. Alfred Prufrock

S'io credesse che...ti rispondo – this Italian quotation from Dante's *Inferno* translates as: If I believed my answer were being given to someone who could ever return to the world, this flame would shake no more. But since no one has ever returned alive from this depth, if what I hear is true, I will answer you without fear of infamy.

Michelangelo – the famed Italian Renaissance painter and sculptor, Michelangelo Buonarotti (1475-1564)

brought in upon a platter – a reference to John the Baptist who was beheaded; then his head was presented on a plate (Mark 6:25).

the Eternal Footman – a personification of death

Lazarus – Christ raised Lazarus from the dead after three days in the grave.

magic lantern – an early slide projector

Prince Hamlet – the protagonist of Shakespeare's play, Hamlet, a sensitive young man searching for answers

The Waste Land

Nam Sibyllam quidem... – translated from Latin and Greek, it means "I have seen with my own eyes the Sibyl hanging in a jar, and when the boys asked her, 'What do you want?' she answered, 'I want to die.'"

For Ezra Pound *il miglior fabbro* – translated from Italian, it means, "for Ezra Pound the better craftsman"

Starnbergersee – a pristine lake in Germany

Hofgarten – a Munich park or garden, translated "Court Garden"

Bin gar keine Russin...deutsch – translated from German, it means, "I am not Russian at all; I come from Lithuania, I am a real German."

archduke's – the cousin of Countess Marie Larisch

Marie, Marie – Countess Marie Larisch (1858-1940), daughter of Duke Ludwig Wilhelm of Bavaria and Henriette Mendel, an actress; these lines are from the Countess's book *My Past.*

Son of man – Jesus Christ

handful of dust – a reference to Genesis 2:7 when God makes man out of the dust of the earth

Frish weht derWing...weilest du? – translated from German it means, "The wind blows fresh/To the Homeland/My Irish girl/Why are you lingering?"

Oed' und leer das Meer – translated from German it means, "desolate and empty the sea"

wicked pack of cards – Tarot cards, used to tell the future

Belladonna – a beautiful but poisonous flower

Lady of the Rocks...The Hanged Man – Eliot references some actual Tarot cards, but some of the cards he has made up and do not exist in a real deck.

Unreal City – a reference to Baudelaire's poem "The Seven Old Men"

I had not...so many – from Dante's *Inferno*, Canto III

Sighs, short and infrequent, were exhaled – from Dante's *Inferno*,
    Canto IV

Saint Mary Woolnoth – a London Church built in the 12th Century

Mylae – a battle in the first Punic War (260 B.C.)

That corpse...in your garden – a reference to Egyptian mythology. Osiris,
    the god of life, was killed. His body parts were buried in different
    places by Isis, his wife, and grain grew over them.

hypocrite lecteur!—mon semblable,—mon frere! – translated from
    French it means, "Hypocrite reader, my fellow man, my brother"; it is
    from Beaudelaire's book of poetry *Fleurs du Mal*.

II Game of Chess

The Chair...the marble – from Shakespeare's *Antony and Cleopatra*

The change of Philomel...So rudely forced – from Greek mythology;
    Philomela, was raped by Tereus of Thrace. He then cut out her tongue
    so that she would not tell anyone.

Shakespeherian Rag – a ragtime song from a 1912 Ziegfield Follies
    program

HURRY UP PLEASE IT'S TIME – a call made by the bartender in British
    pubs when it is closing time

III. The Fire Sermon

The Fire Sermon – a reference to the Fire Sermon by Buddha, who speaks
    against lusts that harm men

Thames – the river that runs through London

Leman – an ancient word for lover; also the name for Lake Geneva

Sweeney to Mrs. Porter – two poetic characters created by T.S. Eliot

Et, O ces...la coupole! – translated from French it means, "And oh, the
    sound of children, singing in the cupola"

Tereu – Tereus, King of Thrace, from Ovid's *Metamorphoses,* who raped his
    sister-in-law

Metropole – London or Paris, the central city (Metropolis)

Tiresias – (Tereu) from Ovid's *Metamorphoses*

Magnus Martyr – Christopher Wren, a famous London architect, who
    recreated the church known as St. Magnus-the-Martyr, which was
    burned in the 1666 London fire

Greenwich, Highbury, Richmond, Kew, Moorgate – places in and around
    London, that were familiar to Eliot

Isle of Dogs – an island in London

Weialala leia – possibly Eliot's onomatopoeia for bells ringing

Elizabeth and Leicester – Queen Elizabeth I of England and one of her court favorites Robert Dudley, the Earl of Leicester

Margate Sands – a place on the southern coast of South Africa; T.S. Eliot went there to recuperate from a nervous breakdown, and he wrote part of "The Waste Land" there.

Carthage – a city in North Africa from St. Augustine's *Confessions*

IV. Death By Water

─────

V. What the Thunder Said

If there were water/...And also water – a Biblical allusion to God's commanding Moses to get water from the rocks (Exodus 17:5-6); Numbers 20:8)

Who is the third...beside you? – a Biblical reference to Christ on the road to Emmaus in Luke 24

Co co rico co co rico – the French version of cock-a-doodle-doo

Ganga – the sacred river of India, the Ganges

Himavant – having to do with snow; the Hindu god of snow; the Himalayan Mountains

Datta...Dayadhvam...Damyata – translated it means, "give, sympathize, control"; this comes from a Hindu fable.

Coriolanus – the exiled king in Shakespeare's play of the same name

Poi s'ascose nel foco che gli affina – translated from Italian it means, "he hid himself in the fire which refines them" from Dante's *Purgatorio*

Quando fiam uti chelidon – translated from Italian it means, "When shall I be like the swallow?"

Le Prince d'Aquitaine a la tour abolie – from the French poem by Gerard de Nerval (1808-1855) "El Desdichado," which translated means, "The prince of Aquitaine whose tower is destroyed"

Hieronymo's mad againe – from Thomas Kyd's *Spanish Tragedy*. Hieronymo stages a play where murderers in various roles are actually killed in revenge for his son's death.

Shantih shantih shantih – a set of words that are not able to be accurately translated; T.S. Eliot commented that they roughly mean, "The Peace that passeth understanding" (from the Bible (Philippians 4:7).

When the Year Grows Old

─────

Buffalo Bill's

Buffalo Bill – William F. Cody (1846-1917), the American showman and general

in Just-
——

Her Lips are Copper Wire
——

Portrait of a Boy

Cross – Known as the Southern Cross, it is a constellation seen in the
Southern Hemisphere.

Centaur – a constellation; the Centaur is a creature in Greek mythology
that is half man and half horse.

Harlem (2)
——

Poet to Bigot
——

The Negro Speaks of Rivers

Euphrates – one of two rivers in Iraq

Congo – a central African river, the second longest river in Africa next to
the Nile

Nile – the longest river in Africa, flowing from northern Egypt into
western Africa

Mississippi – the second longest river in the United States, beginning in
Minnesota and flowing into the Gulf of Mexico

New Orleans – the city at the southern tip of the Mississippi River; known
for its various ethnic groups

my dreams, my works, must wait till after hell
——

A Supermarket in California
Walt Whitman – (1819-1892), a 19th century American poet

Garcia Lorca – (1898-1936), a Spanish poet and dramatist

Charon – from Greek mythology, the boatman or ferryman who transported people to Hades

Lethe – a river in Hades from Greek and Roman mythology; anyone who drinks from it would forget the past.

The Whistle
Loretta Lynn – (b.1934), a popular country music songwriter and singer

8 Fragments for Kurt Cobain
Pills and powders – illegal street drugs

Lucifer's – Satan, the angel in heaven who rebelled against God

monkey – a slang term for a burden; it is often used to refer to heroin addiction.

into a coma in Roma – Cobain overdosed in Rome but survived the experience.

Bellinni or Rafael's Portraits – probably a reference to Vincenzo Bellini (1801-1835), a Sicilian composer; Raphael (1483-1520), is the Italian Renaissance painter, a contemporary of Michelangelo and DaVinci.

Vocabulary

Note: *Vocabulary words are defined here by how they are used in the poems.*
       Traditional uses of the words may be different.

Upon A Wasp Chilled With Cold
apothecary – pharmacist
capital – the head; top
corporation – the body
chafes – rubs vigorously and roughly
dun – grayish-yellow
encramped – constricted; contracted
enravished – overcome
furred – covered
fustian – an appearance like something woven; grand (It is not obvious
          from the poem which definition is intended.)
precepts – beliefs
shanks – long parts of the body; legs

An Hymn to the Evening
forsook – abandoned; left
placid – tranquil, peaceful
purl – to murmur
sable – dark; black
sceptre – the ruling staff of a monarch
zepher – a breeze

The Star-Spangled Banner
haughty – proud, arrogant
havoc – chaos
hireling – a mercenary
perilous – dangerous
ramparts – fortifications; battle walls
reposes – rests
vauntingly – boastfully

A Visit from St. Nicholas
coursers – fleet reindeer
droll – amusing, funny
luster – shine
sash – a window

Thanatopsis
abodes – homes
blight – an affliction
communion – a joining of
eloquence – a moving emotion
hoary – white haired; old
innumerable – unable to be counted
insensible – unresponsive, inert
list – to listen
musings – thoughts, meditations
pall – despair
pensive – thoughtful, meditative
scourged – beaten
seers – wise men, sages
sepulchre – a tomb
shroud – a cloth used to cover a corpse for burial
sustained – assisted, helped
swain – a farmer
treads – walks
vales – a valley
venerable – respected; revered

Paul Revere's Ride
aghast – horrified
alders – types of trees
belfry – the part of a tower where the bells are kept
fleet – fast
gilded – gold-covered; having the appearance of gold
girth – the width of
grenadiers – soldiers
impetuous – forceful
moorings – anchored places
muster – a gathering
sentinel – a guard
spectral – ghostly
stealthy – silent, secretive
weathercock – a weathervane in the shape of a rooster

The Children's Hour
banditti – a bandit
grave – serious, somber
moulder – to decay

scaled – climbed
turret – a tower

The Village Blacksmith
bellows – a machine that pumps air into a fire
brawny – muscular
repose – rest, sleep
sexton – a church official in charge of maintaining the property
sinewy – strong, powerful
toiling – working
wrought – made, created; formed

The Wreck of the Hesperus
brine – salt water; sea water
flaw – *[archaic]* wind
stark – desolate
steed – a horse
stove – broke apart
veering – changing direction suddenly

Barbara Frietchie
bier – a place for the body at a funeral
dame – a woman in charge of a household
horde – an army or large group of people
rebel – southern
spires – pointed church steeples

Annabel Lee
coveted – desired
dissever – to cut off, remove

The Bells
affright – fear
alarum – a warning
brazen – brass; loud
clamorous – loud, noisy
compels – forces
crystalline – sparkling; clear
ditty – a song
ebbs – lessens; moves back
endeavor – a task
euphony – harmonious sound

expostulation – a revelation; disclosure
ghouls – evil spirits
gloats – delights, revels
impels – forces
jangling – clanking, clattering
knells – mournful ringing
monody – a singular sound
monotone – a singular sound that continues without changing
paean – exceeding joy; praise
palpitating – irregularly beating; fluttering, quivering
resolute – unyielding, determined
tintinnabulation – a ringing sound
turbulency – wildness
voluminously – largely, amply
wells – swells, intensifies
wrangling – battling

The Raven
beguiling – enticing
craven – a coward
crest – feathers on the top of a bird's head
decorum – dignity
dirges – funeral songs
ebony – black
gaunt – stark, thin
gloated – shone brightly
mien – manner
obeisance – an act of homage or respect
ominous – ill-omened; gloomy
placid – serene, tranquil
quaff – to drink quickly
quaint – old-fashioned
raven – a large, black crow; another word for the color black
respite – rest
surcease – to stop
undaunted – fearless
ungainly – awkward

To Helen
agate – a shiny, semi-precious, striped stone
wont – accustomed

Old Ironsides
ensign – a flag
threadbare – worn and barely held together by the remaining threads of
        fabric
vanquished – defeated

The Chambered Nautilus
bark – a ship
feign – to pretend
forlorn – abandoned
irised – shining; made iridescent
venturous – adventurous

I Knew A Man By Sight
converse – a conversation
starting – being surprised
mess – food
simultaneously – at the same time
wight – a person

Gettysburg
ampler – more than sufficient
impious – unholy
ire – anger, rage
transfigured – changed, altered
trebled – tripled

from Song of Myself
abased – lowered in esteem
abeyance – a suspension or a lapse
acquisitive – desiring to have something
adjunct – an attachment
athwart – across
boughs – tree limbs
complacent – indifferent; satisfied
disposition – personality; belief
distillation – purification
eddies – swirls
equanimity – equality
exaltations – breathing out
fathomed – without end or bottom

fratricidal – related to the killing of a brother
haughty – proud, arrogant
hieroglyphic – picture writing
impalpable – not able to be felt
inception – a beginning, start
kelson – a reinforcing beam
linguists – people who study language
manifold – many
peruse – to examine
procreant – creative; productive
reckon'd – (reckoned) thought
tenacious – steadfast
trippers – tourists, travelers

<u>I Hear America Singing</u>
blithe – carefree
robust – hearty; vigorous

<u>O Captain! My Captain!</u>
rack – the stress of the storm

<u>When I Heard the Learn'd Astronomer</u>
mystical – mysterious

<u>The Battle Hymn of the Republic</u>
burnished – polished
vintage – wine

<u>Because I could not stop for Death</u>
civility – manners; consideration
cornice – an ornamental molding
surmised – supposed, thought

<u>Hope is the thing with Feathers</u>
abash – to humiliate
gale – a storm
sore – distressful

<u>I can wade grief</u>
balm – comfort

I died for beauty
brethren – brothers
kinsmen – relatives; people having the same experience

I heard a fly buzz when I died
heaves – surges, swellings

I never saw a moor
chart – a map
heather – shrubs
moor – an English field with swamps

I'm nobody! Who are you?
livelong – entire, whole

Success is Counted Sweetest
nectar – a sweet drink

Romeo and Juliet
masquerade – a costume party

A Morning Fancy
apace – quickly, rapidly
azure – blue
fray – a fight
eerie – strange
hovel – a hut; poor dwelling
naught – nothing
nether – lower
opaquer – impenetrable
pellucid – transparent
primal – original
profound – depth; greatness
translucent – clear
unfathomed – unknown

The New Colossus
brazen – brass
refuse – garbage (meaning undervalued people)
teeming – over-populated, crowded
wretched – miserable, dejected

A Caged Bird
chide – to scold, blame
deceit – imitation
piteous – worthy of pity
plaintive – sad, mournful
provision – stored food
unpunctual – delayed, overdue
wistful – sad, longing

The Bumblebee
slouchy – lazy; careless

When the Frost is on the Punkin
mock – to imitate

Solitude
gall – bitterness, sadness
lordly – grand
mirth – laughter; joy
nectared – sweet, delicious
woe – problems, grief

In War-Time (An American Homeward-Bound)
serene – calm

Tears
bards – poets
betwixt – between
wisp – a small strand

America the Beautiful
alabaster – white
impassioned – forceful
strife – difficulties

Casey at the Bat
doffed – lifted
fraud – a cheater
spheroid – a round item (the baseball)
visage – the face; appearance
writhing – twisting

When Ol' Sis' Judy Pray
salvation – delivery from sin

Aner Clute
——

Hodd Putt
unwittingly – accidentally

Homer Clapp
bays – brown horses
revival – a religious meeting or gathering
spanking – precise, exact

The Hill
babbles – talks ceaselessly
boozer – a drinker; an alcoholic
brothel – a house of prostitution
thwarted – rejected
venerable – revered, respected

A Litany of Atlanta
beseech – to ask; pray
blasphemous – profane, non-religious
chaste – pure
cozenage – trickery
debauched – morally corrupted
despot – a tyrant, oppressor
front – to confront, face
guile – slyness
hearsed – carried; buried
hypocrisy – saying one thing and doing another
iniquity – sin
leagued – united
leer – to look lustfully
maimed – crippled, hurt, injured
mockery – the act of making fun of something
pittance – a small amount
ravished – raped
sate – to satisfy
seers – wise men

shackled – chained
travail – anguish
whither – where

<u>Miniver Cheevy</u>
albeit – even though; despite
assailed – raged against
incessantly – continuously
renown – fame
scorn – disdain
vagrant – a wanderer, vagabond

<u>Richard Cory</u>
imperially – regally

<u>A man adrift on a slim spar</u>
adrift – floating
crest – the peak
incessant – constant, continuous
seething – teeming, heaving
spar – mast
tumult – commotion, turmoil

<u>A man said: "Thou tree!"</u>
––––

<u>I stood upon a high place</u>
carousing – reveling

<u>In the desert</u>
bestial – brutish, animal-like

<u>Should the wide world roll away</u>
essential – necessary, needed

from <u>War is Kind</u>
shroud – a cloth used to cover a corpse for burial

<u>Lift Ev'ry Voice and Sing</u>
chastening – punishing, disciplining
resound – to echo, reverberate

The Creation
barren – empty
spangling – adorning, covering
spat – spit

Misapprehension
fortitude – strength; ability
imbued – filled; soaked
subdued – quieted; calmed
tremulously – with vibrations

We Wear the Mask
guile – deceit; cunning
myriad – many; multitudinous
subtleties – devious tricks

Harvest Moon
dune – a mound
sodden – soaked, saturated
teeming – swarming, crowded
writhe – to struggle

Harvest Moon: 1916
famished – extremely hungry
gropes – fumbles; feels
harken – to listen
legions – depths
perpetual – never ending
shrouding silver – covering of the moon

Madonna of the Evening Flowers
spire – a pinnacle, point

The Cyclists
careening – moving rapidly forward in an uncontrolled manner
carrion – dead, decaying bodies
exultant – jubilant, triumphant
foreboding – a bad omen, fear
pinions – wings
tainted – polluted
virile – strong, powerful

The Cremation of Sam McGee
derelict – a deserted ship
grisly – horrible
grub – food
hearkened – listened closely
loathed – hated
moil – to work
raved – spoke wildly
spent – exhausted
trice – moment

The Death of the Hired Man
beholden – obligated
broken – worn out
daft – crazy about; enthusiastic
eaves – the overhang of a roof
grudge – to deny
harbour – (harbor) to give shelter to; to take in
musing – thinking; meditating
piqued – pricked, annoyed
queer – strange; unusual
taut – tight

Fire and Ice
———

The Road Not Taken
diverged – separated
hence – since
wanted – desired, lacked

Two Tramps in Mud Time
alight – to land on
avocation – a hobby
cloven – divided
twain – two
vernal – springtime
vocation – a job
I Sit and Sew
holocaust – total destruction
idle – not active
futile – useless

ken – understanding; knowledge
martial – warlike
panoply – full array
roseate – optimistic
stifles – smothers

Grandmither, think not I forget
grope – to search
kirkyard – a church cemetery
rue – a yellow flower with bitter-smelling leaves
thyme – a shrub

Chicago
cunning – cleverness
magnetic – fascinating; compelling
toil – to work
wanton – cruel; excessive

Chicago Poet
——

Fog
haunches – the back half of an animal

Grass
——

Shenandoah
——

Smoke
——

General William Booth Enters Into Heaven
blear – ragtag, shabby
bravoes – murderers
countenance – the facial expression or manner of conducting oneself
dank – damp
drabs – prostitutes
mouldy – rotting
fanatical – fervent, zealous

havoc – chaos
lame – injured
legions – masses; a large group of soldiers
lepers – people who are avoided or ignored
queer – strange; unusual
raiment – uniforms; clothing
sages – wise, respectable men
salvation – delivery from sin
throng – a large group
sibyls – wise, respectable women
transcendent – divine
unabated – relentless
vixens – wicked women
vermin-eaten – bug-invested

The Emperor of Ice-Cream
affix – to attach
concupiscent – desirous
curds – chunks
dawdle – to linger, loiter
dumb – unable to speak
embroidered – attached fancily
fantails – a type of decoration
wenches – servant or country girls

Let Me Live Out My Years
grisly – grim, dreadful
heyday – the peak; the best time

The Red Wheelbarrow
——

This Is Just to Say
——

I Shall Not Care
bough – a branch of a tree

The Kiss
——

The Proud Poet
consolation – comfort
disdain – scorn
mirth – laughter; joy
orators – speakers
perilous – dangerous
score – twenty
smart – to sting
stern – strict

Trees
intimately – closely

Oread
——

I Have a Rendezvous with Death
rendezvous – a meeting, an appointment

The Love Song of J. Alfred Prufrock
deferential – polite
etherized – sedated; passed out
insidious – devious, deceptive
malingers – pretends to be sick
meticulous – precise; careful
scuttling – scurrying
obtuse – simple-minded; stupid
tedious – tiresome; dull

The Waste Land
aethereal – eerie
asserted – added
beneficent – kind, benevolent
carbuncular – having sores; infected
carious – decayed
cisterns – water tanks
coffered – decorated
colonnade – – rows of columns
currants – fruit similar to raisins
demobbed – discharged
demotic – ordinary; daily

digress – to wander off the topic
divan – a couch
dugs – breasts
endeavours – (endeavors) tries
fortnight – fourteen days
gammon – ham, bacon
garret – an attic
gentile – a Christian
gramophone – an early record player
inexplicable – not able to be explained
inviolable – unbreakable, unchallenged
laquearia – a statue (used for protection of a house)
lamentation – weeping
mince – to divide
musing – thinking
nymphs – spirits
patronizing – treating someone with disrespect
profusion – an abundance
propitious – favorable
prudence – judgment
reminiscent – recollecting
reverberation – echoing
solicitor – a lawyer
supine – horizontal; flat
sylvan – wooded, forest
trams – streetcars
tubers – underground plants; root plants
unguent – an ointment
wrought – filled

When the Year Grows Old
boughs – tree branches
melancholy – sadness, depression

Buffalo Bill's
defunct – dead, deceased
queer – strange; unusual

in Just-
————

Her Lips are Copper Wire
incandescent – burning, flaming
insulate – covered; protected

Portrait of a Boy
affronting – facing
aldermen – city officials
blurts – spots
doubloons – old Spanish money
froth – trivial
galleon's – a sailing ship's
gemmed – colored
motes – specks, particles
syenite – a light-colored rock
wattled – having folds of skin under the chin (wattles)

Harlem (2)
deferred – delayed, hindered
fester – to decay, rot

Poet to Bigot
meagre – (meager) inadequate, skimpy

The Negro Speaks of Rivers
dusky – dark

my dreams, my works, must wait till after hell
dregs – remains
puny – weak, small

A Supermarket in California
absurd – ridiculous, foolish
grubber – a sloppy person; scrounger
enumerations – listings
odyssey – a journey
penumbras – shadows

The Whistle

corrugated – ridged, grooved
fulvous – orange-brown –
pneumatic – filled
scrotum – a container
sonorous – resounding
syncopation – the beat; accent
throttled – regulated the movement or engines
titanous – huge; metallic
winch – a crank

8 Fragments for Kurt Cobain

crevice – pleasant memories
incognito – being in disguise
libido – the sex drive
placate – to pacify, assuage
remorseless – merciless
reverberating – echoing
riff – a musical phrase; melody
synchronicity – the occurrence of two events at the same time
threshold – the edge

Index by Author

Index by Title or First Line